Andrew Fusek Peters has written many books for all ages, including novels, poetry and plays. Before becoming a full-time writer, he was the arts correspondent for the television series *Heart of the Country*. Today, Andrew lives and works in Shropshire. Passionate about the British countryside, he is addicted to the pleasures of wild swimming and photography. *Dip* features luminous black and white photographs taken by him and his daughter, Rosalind.

dip

Wild Swims from the Borderlands

Andrew Fusek Peters

LONDON · SYDNEY · AUCKLAND · JOHANNESBURG

1 3 5 7 9 10 8 6 4 2

First published in 2014 by Rider, an imprint of Ebury Publishing
Ebury Publishing is a Random House Group company

This paperback edition published by Rider in 2015

Text copyright © 2014 by Andrew Fusek Peters

The Random House Group Limited Reg. No. 954009
Addresses for companies within the Random House Group can be found at

www.randomhouse.co.uk

A CIP catalogue record for this book is available from the British Library

Penguin Random House is committed to a sustainable future for
our business, our readers and our planet. This book is made from
Forest Stewardship Council® certified paper.

MIX
Paper from
responsible sources
FSC
www.fsc.org   FSC® C018179

Printed and bound in Great Britain by Clays Ltd, St Ives plc

ISBN 9781846044489

Copies are available at special rates for bulk orders. Contact the sales
development team on 020 7840 8487 for more information.

To buy books by your favourite authors and register for offers, visit
www.randomhouse.co.uk

Please note: this book is a personal account and should not be used as a substitute for expert guidance on wild swimming. Neither the author nor the publisher can be held responsible for any loss or claim arising from the use or misuse of the information in this book. For advice on wild swimming safety, please consult dedicated websites such as www.wildswimming.co.uk

Contents

'...that earth was better than gold, and that water,
every drop of it, was a precious jewel. And that these
were great and living treasures. And that all riches
whatsoever else was dross in comparison.'

Thomas Traherne, *Centuries of Meditation*

Introduction

FOR ME, THE URGE TO SWIM OUTDOORS in wild water is a compulsion; one that has led me out into the hills and valleys of Shropshire and Wales, in every season, for more than two decades. My wife, Polly, and I moved to her adopted home county of Shropshire on a whim that coincided with us getting married. Twenty-three years later, we're still here in the borderlands of the Marches, the roots of family, friends and community digging ever deeper.

I grew up in London, though even as a kid I yearned for the untamed and the uncultivated. During my teens I took up long-distance running, catching trains to the far edges of the city so that I could pound my way back. Often I would run in the evening, revelling in the rhythm of legs and feet creating their own current to flow across parkland and lit suburb and on through the neon spills of night. So perhaps it's no surprise that he who sought wild edges should find himself living in an in-between place, a meandering border county where myth, history and landscape rise, fall and blur.

During our time together, Polly has often described our walks as being like taking a stroll with a Labrador retriever or English Setter, with me sniffing out any opportunity to bound into water. Pond, lake, stream, river, tarn, sea: if it's clean and safe-looking, there's no point loitering and looking, I want to get in it. Our two children have grown up watching Dad dunk, dive and douse, and often they'll join me, though not in winter or early spring. They, like Polly, are more clement-weather dippers, but for me the insistent tug is year-round.

When *Waterlog* by Roger Deakin was published in 2000, I knew I'd found a guru, one I thank many times when I wade out from a swimming spot, glowing all over with good feeling. His wild-water Bible of a book traced his route around Britain through submersion. But the map of his watery journey appeared to miss the Marches – the contours of which I've taken great pleasure in exploring since I began calling them home. What a treat, to map out my own maze of dips and delvings, of watering holes that have yielded up their secrets.

What is the appeal of wild water? Swimming outdoors in Britain is always going to be a chilly experience whatever the weather, and for me, it's not about exercise: as the title of this book suggests, I may not spend a long time submerged. I can't always see the bottom; am not always sure at what point I might pass out of my depth, but I'm still compelled.

When I was a child, my mum would take me and my brother to Berkshire, where we'd all swim in the Thames. Diving in held the thrill of faint danger and, beyond fear, immersion. All of summer was contained in the promise of the far bank where I clambered out, sleek as an otter, nose sniffing the far country. I knew then what I know now. This is the water that heals, restores, fills me with glow-worm gladness. So that was the start, a practice imbibed from my mother who had grown up in land-locked Czechoslovakia. No seaside for her; her childhood summer holidays and weekend jaunts were spent by rivers and lakes. It's an inherited pattern I've woven into my own roamings the length and breadth of Britain and beyond. Always, wherever I am, there's the lure of finding the other-ness of immersion in the landscape.

My longing for water will see me questioning people as to their local plunge pools, or poring over Ordnance Survey maps, tracing tiny lanes and footpath lines to see where they intersect with anything blue. I'm a water-optimist in that I carry trunks and towel on most outings, just in case. I also generally have old sandals to hand to minimise the chances of gashed feet.

When I do alight on a new, promising site, all sorts of instincts cut in to establish whether I think it looks safe and palatable to dip into: what sort of water-life is around and in it? If it's good enough for minnows or aerating aquatic weeds, it's good enough for me. How does it smell? How does it look? Is there any don't-swim-here-indicative algae? How deep is it? Can I see strong currents? If not, but I think there might be some lurking, is there a slow-moving stretch where the level will be lower than my shoulders? Can I get in and out easily? Then there are my own rules of no impact: no rubbish (collect any that others have left and take it away); don't disturb water birds; don't pick anything; avoid breaking or harming water plants; observe the Countryside Code. All common sense.

So, to *Dip* and a year of wild swimming through every month of the year, which begins with joyful January duckings. When I first began thinking about putting together a collection of swims, submersions and explorations that would radiate out from around my home, to further afield, I was still recovering from a six-month stretch of severe depression that had seen me hospitalised for part of the time. During those long months, writing, reading, swimming, laughing, the taste of food, love, activity, the outdoors: all were inaccessible; terrifying; gone. As I slowly mended, it was

And the River Loves Me

I love the river and
The river loves me
Down by the Clun
At Clunbury.

Climb the gate
Of the village hall,
Oh follow me son
And follow me all.

Skirting fields
By hem and hedge,
Then over the fence
To a gravelly edge;

A jungle of alder
And nettles that sway,
Keen to sting those
Who brush past this way.

Beyond is the water,
Her song and her swerve
Held by the clay
In a tight-fisted curve.

Just as we dare
To dive with a splash,
Out of the shadows
A wallowing crash,

As something, yes something
Leaps out of the Clun,
All sleek and wet-heaving,
One blink and he's gone.

And all that he's left
Are his prints in the mud,
The echo of otter
Stirring our blood.

Oh for the magic,
The bright mystery
As we dip in the Clun
At Clunbury.

ANDREW FUSEK PETERS

january

River Cwamnantcol

Nantcol Falls, Wales

THIS IS A DAY OF RECONFIGURATION, where the mist has wiped the sea from the very face of the earth and the sun is swaddled far from the reach of human eye. A mist like this drains perspective from landscape. It sucks sound from our surroundings, until our car is a soft swish brushing over the coast road, before we turn inland at the village of Llanbedr. My wife drives while I navigate and our son and daughter play the old game of making words out of licence-plate letters, though the other cars that pass us are few and far between in this out-of-season emptiness. Lanes dart through dark woods of twisted oak, carrying us higher, in search of the river's bubbling beginning – and a campsite car park. It's almost entirely empty when we pull up, aside from signs to remind the unwary walker not to stray too close to the sheer, rocky edges. For good reason.

If ever there was a day for ghosts, this is it. The rope swing above the swollen river current is empty and still. The wildlife-extolling information plaques are covered in a dew of drizzle. On a stone wall, perfectly perched for the camera I do not have in my hand, a buzzard eyes us as uncommon interlopers. I love the breadth of this big bird; most British of raptors, the sense of weight and hidden width in her haunches. To oblige us, she unfurls, gains the air: layered brown wings a brief blossoming when all around is hunkered down.

The water beyond the campsite edge splays out, rushing, overblown, a song that speaks verse after verse of endless winter rains. The path running alongside diverts suddenly and cuts into the hill away from cruel and slippery drops. It is delineated by huge planks of oak wedged into the ground, with iron staves, a

4

rough staircase that goes against the grain. We climb and to our right the river squeezes between small canyons of stone. It leaps, pools, froths urgently. On the surface of one of these pools lie three perfect circles of viscous foam that jostle each other, like squashed beach balls or leaden smoke rings.

We follow, further, higher. *Here?* I wonder, or maybe *here*, though my mind is filled with calculation. Would the weight of water carry me away like so much panicky flotsam, or duck me under in those roiling whirlpools? The rules have changed. Where summer decrees a diving-in spot, or a little light wallowing, winter has come and submerged such easy undertakings. Add in the cold and lack of sunlight and it's common sense all the way: I must aim higher up. The trees on either side – sycamore, oak and alder – are bent almost double, as if they know that winds will come and they must be prepared. I feel I'm in a forest of bonsai; like Alice, I have downed the draft that says 'Drink Me' and am unexpectedly the height of a house. The branches are bare, yet flower with a lichen that is verdant in its scabby greenness.

Beyond the trees, we reach a stony plateau where the river has calmed itself into a series of gentle meanders. *Here!* I whisper to myself, recognising a spot from some summers ago. This was where my friend David and I had stripped down to our swimming trunks, much to the amusement of our respective families, waded in, busily dipped heads under and larked around like a pair of teenagers. There's a photo of David beached on a giant middle-of-the-river rock like some hairy, small whale. That golden afternoon, water had gone about its work, loosening the stresses of everyday and lubricating our shrill laughter.

Here! I finally decide, reaching for that echo of a far summer. The waterproof jacket comes off to play its role as groundsheet for my undressing. Strangely, the horizontal, drifting drizzle does not bother me. Once my trunks are on, there is no pause for bravery before I cantilever off across the smooth, pebbly scree that gives access to a water dark with dim-lit sky. I splash towards the rock that David and I marked with our bodies, and find beneath my feet enough depth to lower myself carefully into the river. I let go and sink down. The shock is unspeakable. It is January after all, the new year only just emerging from the cocoon of Christmas. The Christmas Eve Wiener Schnitzel and the twirling candle-powered brass angels of my Czech forefathers are not long behind us. Always, as a child, I loved these delicate, poised creatures circling round and round, fuelled by no more than the invisible currents of heat. At home, the cards still hang in ranks along the living-room ceiling. This is entirely the wrong end of the season, when hibernation is the yearning of anyone with sense.

But still, I am here now, fully awake, delving into the river as if to find its future, warmer dreaming. I have had decades of this immersion and now my body shrugs as if to say, 'Really? Again? Oh well, you may as well get on with it...' My mind, however, is another matter, urging me with all evolutionary instinct to flee. At least I am in the water. Not so long ago, when depression had me in its grip, water was the foe I could not even approach, let alone jump into. The only current I felt the drag of was negativity, the only safe submersion, my bed and the sinking down of medicated sleep. But not today. As I shriek and scramble back to shore and warmth, there is a fizz that is – just maybe – the gift of Nantcol. For all that energy, that skyward, rain-ward descent, that sluicing-through of every brook and burn, that call of the far-off sea, that careering round corners, down canyons, that falling, that fluidity, that impelled, compelling acceleration – for one second, all of it is in me and through me and by me again.

And although the day is damp and the cold rain is scribbling zigzags through the air, and grey is not a colour but the appellation of whole months that have been and are still to come, I feel synaptic, almost giddy with stars, my limbic brain coursing with ideas; banks and boundaries breached and flooded with language and life.

Colemere, Shropshire

JANUARY CALLS TO ME, after days of torrent, when the media warn that roads will be washed away and that rivers shall burst their banks. Even as Polly and I head north past Shrewsbury towards Shropshire's flatter fenlands, there is a rumour that the River Severn might break free, despite man's preventative defences. However, these stories of doom and flood appear insubstantial within the clarity of light today, a startling sun that gladdens any wintry heart.

I have visited the glacial meres in the north of our county only once in twenty-two years. This trip is to be my remedy. It's still holiday season and the roads bear the Shropshire equivalent of a full-on traffic jam – at least three cars in front of us, and one single truck, manage to make our striking northwards grindingly slow. At last, we turn off the main Ellesmere road and into winding lanes that thread through a shining landscape. The first pool we see is not the best display of what the area has to offer, being overlooked by a towering rubbish tip. This small weedy run-off is denuded of tree and shrub, dressed only by a rising and falling fringe of greedy gulls; I shall not be swimming here. Then it's

Colemere

behind us as we skirt filled-in gravel pits, pass the flat, jewelled plate of Whitemere and find the car park that edges Colemere. This is more like it.

Colemere Lake is large, half a mile across, and ringed with woods that hide a well-maintained walkway. It's owned by Shropshire County Council but managed by the Shropshire Wildlife Trust in association with several other environmental organisations. I can hear my inner guidebook voice as I scan the view, underneath which is the whisper that this is the kind of spot I am normally wary of. The car park is full and there's a sprinkling of wellied-up families, dog-walkers and buggy-pushers out on a flat woodland jaunt around the water. It all looks a bit too tidy to me and I begin to withdraw my earlier promise, which committed me to trunks and dip. My wife simply smiles that knowing smile of hers as we head into the woods to follow the signposted path, as if she knows how I live for wavering indecision.

Light tilts through the trees, and further along are a couple standing under a smooth, towering beech, their small son pointing upwards. Their baby grins from a front sling carrier and we all pause, listening hard. There's a swooping, melodic, repeated single note. Up comes my lens once the dad has pointed out the source, and there is a nuthatch, perched high on a broken stump of branch. After a couple of clicks, the bird flies and the little boy, Alfie, tells us about the wren they've also spotted today. While we stand here chatting, I scroll back on my camera screen and find that the best part in our simple exchange isn't me capturing the flash of orange and streak of nuthatch-New-Romantic eye shadow, but it is showing it to this small boy and listening to his excitement at seeing it close-up.

We stride on and, by now, I'm getting itchy. The woods are all very well, but where can I access the water? My rising frustration at not actually being able to see the lake isn't helped when we do find a few small bights or bays and look into water that is a thick, green puree of soup. It's a chlorotic scum: a yearly green-algae bloom known as 'the breaking of the meres', the word 'breaking' borrowed from the breaking of the yeast on beer-in-the-making. It accurately describes the off-putting vivid green froth floating in front of us. There is some debate among the Shropshire Wildlife Trust about how natural it is, and there is no record of the froth appearing before the beginning of dairy farming, with all the associated run-off. Whatever its origin, I don't wish to wear a fluorescent plankton overcoat. We step back and I state firmly that I'm not going in.

However, halfway around, the trees peter out and there's a gently shelving beach. The sun is still slanting down and the water here appears fresh, clean and clear. I can actually see the bottom, and it's not even muddy, it's sandy.... I perform a quick about-turn from my earlier no-swim complaining and whip out my towel, though the constant perambulation behind me makes me feel like I'm changing in an airport corridor. According to research, the nearest Least Water Lily patch is a hundred yards away. This is the only site in the country where it grows, making Colemere a Site of Special Scientific Interest (SSSI), the highest level of protection available in the UK. I have no desire to mess with this seriously rare species, though am starting to feel like one myself – the only wild swimmer foolish enough to hit the Meres of North Shropshire so soon after Christmas. The sight of me standing knee deep in the water certainly raises a few cheers from the small crowd that has gathered. Pride now forces me onwards as my toes remind me that it *is* January, it's *very* January and that hanging about could be medically harmful. At least the recent snow has retreated.

I take a deep breath and listen out for the bells of Colemere, said to come from a drowned monastery, but the only sound is the distant honk of Canada geese and children's whoops echoing among the beech trees. Then I'm in and swimming towards the vast flocks of greylag, goldeneye and pochard. I know the greylag is never going to have birders frothing at the mouth, but I love the cheerful orange of its beak, and its surprising grace as it flaps through the sky despite its bulk. For a moment, I am one of them, a clumsy, wading water bird, being snapped by my camera-bearing wife as I crest and immerse myself into this nature-born sinkhole. Years of winter swims have given me the willpower to ignore my body's primal response, but this is still not going to be a marathon. I swim out briefly, turn, head for the comfort of shore and even as I step, dripping, from the mere, I know that reticence could have so easily bidden me ignore all the delights of water and swap them for the blast of a car heater. I know also that, whether it's adrenaline or pure physiology, a walk that had seemed somewhat dull has been transformed into the excitement of the new. Even the year ahead, only recently birthed, fills with possibility and potential. I feel ridiculously positive, almost giggly. The woods on the way back have turned brighter, the coots that bob on the water more defined, and I even banter with the tribe of pensioners in superbly expensive walking kit who ask me if I have warmed up yet.

As we loop right round in full circle, I tell Polly some of the history and information I uncovered as I researched this swim-hole the night before. For we are walking through a two-hundred-million-year-old desert. And we are also at the meeting point of two huge ice sheets long, long after that: one that moved down from Scotland and the Lake District by way of the Irish Sea, the other creeping along from mountainous North Wales, both bringing rock and stone and sediment. But above all, these glaciers brought themselves and it is the nature of glaciers to 'calve' at the edges: for the vast cliff faces to crack and crumble and for huge masses of ice to break away.

When I was a young man, I travelled with my brother to the far reaches that lay high above a Swiss valley. Marc and I dared to scramble right towards the edge of the ice, despite the danger of vast slabs slipping off and flattening us. Our goal was simple. The Swiss locals sourced much of their quartz crystals from these vertiginous heights. All it took was tomfoolery and, at the age of eighteen, I had plenty. I remember the air cooling metre by metre, until we reached the point where suddenly shorts were not adequate and the great looming mountain of ice lost its beauty and gave off a more terrifying aspect. We scooped out what we could from the surrounding white rocks – tiny clusters of gleaming quartz that no New Age shop would deem worthy, except that we were now our own hunters and gatherers and this compression of light was justly earned. My brother, with whom I bathed in the crystal-clear stream water that gushed from the base of the glacier, has long gone into the dark valleys of grief. He is part of another geological drift, but I have those crystals still to fleck my mind and memory as well as the imagined sound of the glacier calving by night, a multiplication and mix-up of thunder and lightning that roared into our dreams.

Today, I still feel close to the rivers of ice. The depths of Colemere were caused by one giant, calved – broken-off – iceberg, left behind to settle in the great fields of glacial drift like a blank and lonely orphan. Abandoned, melting, causing the kettle hole beneath to be filled later by streams and the second largest aquifer in the UK. This is Colemere: stillness born of movement and drama.

I'm eager to return to these meres, to explore, to seek out some of the quieter spots, perhaps on a June evening when the Brown Hawker dragonfly is set on her dance, but certainly some spot were I might (selfishly) have all this glacier gift and drift to myself. If the water is just right, I'll also endeavour to be braver, swim further, dawdle, take my time, not be in a rush to be free of the clutches of dusk and the coming night. But today, I'm content, glad with this rare excursion to the north of the county, happy and hungry for lunch.

Walcot Estate

across the middle of one of the lakes. There are still long-time villagers who claim their own or a distant family member's sighting. And why does she walk on water? Because she is a ghost from the time before, when these very depths were still land. To her – this echo of a centuries-old wraith – water is no barrier to a constitutional stroll. As for the second part of the tale, during the Second World War, when the Royal Army Ordnance Corps was billeted at Walcot, it's said that various of the men stationed there would refuse to take the 'lady-walk' by night. All for fear of what some claimed they had seen: the drifting figure of a woman, dressed all in white, moving along the path. Rumour, whisper, speculation, mistaken identity.... It's a story that expands and contracts, much as the fog over water. Some say she was a jilted lover, others that a man with his eyes on the inheritance strangled his wife on their wedding day, which explains the white dress.

Whatever her tale, I have never met with the lady, despite many hundreds of visits at dawn, day, dusk and sometimes into the evening. And already she slips from my mind, just as the wisps of haze that hang like tufts of sheep's wool are fading. The resident swans and visiting goosander, hooded like floating monks, appear insubstantial in this half-vapour, mere outlines of themselves as they drift and glide on the black waters where night is still held.

We cross the bridge between the lakes and cut through the jumble of converted outbuildings and houses, an almost self-contained hamlet, raised up overlooking the valley. Behind us, the Long Mynd rears its flanks, a frozen, mid-humped Nessie carving valleys as she goes. An ancient ice house yawns a dark mouth to our left, all use swallowed into history, though the walled garden it leans against is being reclaimed through the initiative of the local community. We skirt the high wall and follow the resting sunlight to the beginnings of the arboretum.

I live for these crisp days, when the sky is clean and clear and real winter puts on a show that has nothing to do with the grey fudge we have spent weeks digesting. It opens up the possibility of risk, currently nestled in my backpack and consisting of a towel, a pair of trunks, wetsuit gloves and neoprene 'feet'. Already we have passed through the gnarled apple trees of the old orchard and can see ahead the water that is midway between pond and small lake. I've swum here in October, when the water was fresh, slightly cheeky but not yet an affront to my circulation. Then, there were still dragonflies, eking out the last of late-season warmth. February, with white-fall brightening the frozen mud, is different.

Polly arches her eyebrows, indicating that I might no longer *be* mad, but *am* mad to do this. What can I do but agree, as she holds my bag while I change. One of the many things I love about Shropshire is a general sparseness of people out and about in the landscape, the lack of crowds. Perhaps it's because I grew up in London and, while I enjoy new encounters with fellow walkers, equally I relish those hikes where I don't meet a soul; though perhaps those absent souls are the wise ones: indoors, heating on, enjoying their lack of hypothermia. Here today, it's just us and a quizzical blue tit.

Meanwhile, I'm glad my camera is tucked away in the rucksack. The skinny guy with the goose pimples, gloved and footed, puffing out cold smoke rings, is not a very groovy look. Not that I care too much. I also recall the only comment I've had about swimming in this pool in the past: that 'there are leeches'. Well, I've never climbed out dripping with a tiny slug-vampire attached, and if they have any sense they'll be hibernating. I dip in first one foot, then the other, happy that this is not a squidge-pond or a sedimental sink-station. Underfoot is sure, solid, though the temperature is sudden and shocking. I prance about like a ninny for a few seconds as my wetsuit boots fill and my toes complain, but there's no getting out just yet.

There is something about properly cold water that is both astringent and more real that any hyped-up version of reality TV. This is no bush-tucker trial as I wade in and strike out for the middle of the pond. My body insists loudly that I head back and my mind is utterly convinced that drowning is a looming outcome. My skin is beaten down with water, hammered with temperature, locked in a battle of willpower. And yet, there is this, the core of wild swimming, the simple whoop of it all, the joy that is free and earned with each furious stroke of my arms and push of my legs. The wonderful lines of the great English nature writer Richard Jefferies sometimes rise like bubbles when I'm in water: 'It is eternity now. I am in the midst of it. It is about me in the sunshine; I am in it as the butterfly in the light-laden air. Nothing has to come; it is now. Now is eternity; now is the immortal life.' When water closes around me, this is eternally the moment I am alive. It's a fist-shake at fear, a thrown gauntlet to shadow, a defiance of dread.

Jefferies lost himself in landscape. England was his Eden and its watery aspects are mine also. To swim is to breathe, especially in these dark and dangerous winter months. It's a creative interaction, a compulsive urge; paraphrasing the poet Elizabeth Jennings, it's an act that dares the darkness – again and again and again. It might sound like bravado, but I am defeating fear of death every time I jump in the water.

To dunk or not to dunk? That is the question. There is a

growing panic as I float out of my depth and take in the fact that I am buoyed up by winter. I might well be inhabiting the season and the early year full on, but it's time to acknowledge my shivering limits. Definitely no head-wetting today. I turn and strike out for the bank, clamber up, dripping and steaming, my breath heaving in huge gusts and gouts. I cannot preen myself, releasing oil to waterproof my feathers, have no down to insulate against the day and night. All I own is this Darwinian skin, evolving out of hair and into clothes. From outdoor hunter and caveman to inner-bungalow-sedentary-sapiens. I am not made for this, but as I dip, I am the arrow flying back in time to my ancestral memories. I came from water, I have briefly returned and I feel this elemental urge that drives me on.

Always, always, after every swim – the consequence of gladness that might be part adrenaline. But as the water lifts me, so does the act reflect my interior mood. Though my toes are numb, and my teeth a set of clattering hooves as I towel dry and change, there is a certain jaunt in my step when we turn round to crunch through light snow and retrace our steps.

As if the gods have taken all this lowing sun and pasted it onto their grinning faces, one more piece of blessed luck shines down. I have my camera and there, to the side of the path, landing on a pile of woody brash, is an apparition that is so much more than legend. Fellow village-neighbour Tim is already there with his binoculars and knowledge of how hungry the barn owls are at the moment. Owls hunting by day are not that unusual, he tells me. However, I have walked this drive for year on year and never seen an owl. Now, this magnificent raptor takes off, spreads its significant wings to search out the unploughed strip of field and lets out its characteristic high-pitched shrieks that will flush out

Tributary of Arto

I suggest heading up by Llanbedr to one of our favourite discoveries, the small waterfalls near the great Mordor-like lake of Cym Bychan. Sandwiches are made up with the best that the local supermarket has to offer – pretty good really: Gruyère and rocket on fresh-baked baguettes. Hot Assam tea is brewed and flasked and we're off, all four of us.

The coast road past Barmouth, if you ignore the serried ranks of caravan parks, is a marvel. There is a great sweep of bay that makes up the Lleyn Peninsula. Behind looms the range that includes Snowdon, always held up in shadow as if we might accidentally be witness to a far country we can only dream of. Most visitors have believed the lie that summer is the best season this stretch of Wales has to offer, so the roads are virtually empty. When we turn inland at Llanbedr, the emptiness goes a step further, hollowing out our route, trees long stripped of their leaves. We are the only ones heading up into the mountains. We pass nothing and no one, except for the odd buzzard gliding high above. The road follows the River Artro, echoing it as both begin to narrow. There are fewer passing places and the tarmac begins to wiggle uncomfortably as it squeezes through great glacial boulder fields, every stone gilded in green moss and lichen. The trees are different here – shorter, wind-stunted oaks and ash and alder, mini Pictish forests where I wouldn't be surprised to return by full moon and see what myths merely dream of.

What always amazes me about such 'aspirational' roads is their confidence in following the contours of valley and hill ever higher. The tracks that once supported cart and horse, where drovers walked their Welsh Black cattle, where clogs of farm workers trudged – all have been buried. They leave just an imprint, visible to map makers, helpful foundations for the asphalt that hums under our wheels. Thanks to the track makers, the lengthsmen of old, the way is clear. Without them, this route would be impassable, overgrown rock and grass, and the river a hidden Shangri-La.

There is proper water in the Artro today. Recent rains have made its lower levels a roaring froth that even a mad wild swimmer like me respects and is wary of. This is why our aim has to be higher, where tributaries are unable to throw their weight around or pull any fast, current-bound poses. At last, we cross the tiny bridge of Cae-Hewydd, reach our pull-in and disgorge. As soon as we exit, the cold is upon us. Scarves and hats are pulled low for armour. According to the US Army Survival Manual, you can lose 40 to 45 per cent of body heat from an unprotected head, for the head is a good radiator of heat, and there is a large amount of blood in circulation up there. I always suspected my overactive thinking was exercise. This confirms it.

As I step over the broken stone wall, the first of the river pools is revealed. A waterfall about eight feet high spills into a rocky basin. Nice for a dip in the summer, and the force of water from the falls has proper Jacuzzi-jet properties. But I am a swim-aholic. The first or more obvious spot doesn't always compel me. My spirit generally wants to explore what's round the corner, what gold lies behind the next kink in the way. The footpath takes us and our wellies through squidgy bog. It is the little sister of our road, sticking close to this tributary, doing its best to imitate its curves and bends. A further pool and some more climbing over a landscape of crumbling brown ferns leads us to the well-known place of so many summers. Here is a rocky riverscape, the detritus of the Ice Age sprinkled like boulder-confetti. The river is forced to make do, to duck and dive around such immovable obstacles.

In so doing, there are small but perfectly formed pools and jets of spilling current that form natural whirlpools.

This is the place. The rock is dry enough to sit on. My son and daughter retreat a few years back towards childhood as they construct little homes for imaginary creatures under the earthy overhang. Moss for flooring, dried grass and leaves for walls, river-smoothed pebbles for furniture. I'm enchanted and optimistic that they can so easily return there, that their own golden age isn't yet entirely forgotten.

What I have not forgotten, however, is my relatively recent rise from the great swaddling mist of clinical depression. Today I am a lover of all that is outdoors. Back when I was ill, I hunkered at home or hibernated in my overheated room in a psychiatric hospital. Suddenly, air, seasons, freshness, the very hint of cold were transformed from welcome friend to strange and alien threat. Fear took up residence and convinced me to see the world through his eyes and his eyes alone. During the eight weeks I stayed in two hospitals, I managed to leave the second one only once on my own, near the end of my stay. My walk, in what I would now see as quite pleasant leafy streets, was a particular torture. I passed an empty house, and began to calculate, once I became (inevitably) homeless, whether I could break in there, and how I'd keep warm and feed myself. Once I reached the main, grittier environs of Hagley Road, I took note of several sad-looking B&Bs. In my mind, I was holed up in one of them already, living out of a battered suitcase, hoping to get enough vodka from the offie to find a final oblivion. It sounds melodramatic but at the time it was real, the whole cityscape hostile to my presence. In the small supermarket, I marvelled at people going about their business. They seemed to know what to buy, could make decisions with my late brother's manic depression. Perhaps Big Pharma wasn't actually trying to shut down my mind to all creativity. Maybe they weren't out to dose me up with 'Soma', the state-produced happy drug described in the novel *1984*, so I could dribble through my tranquillised days. And perhaps my appointed counsellor, M, whose wise gifts of listening and words came through the grace of the NHS Community Mental Health Team, was someone with whom I could open up the Pandora's box of my own past. My path to recovery became a surprising team effort: two great psychiatrists (plus one appalling), psychiatric nurses, a supportive visiting Crisis Team, an extraordinary counsellor, a combination of medications that slowly took effect; six crawling months; finally accepting that I was actually, truly ill; CBT/mindfulness training – and all that time, my family, my closest friends and warrior Polly, always, always there. It's a huge list; a very humbling one. And then there's water. Wild water.

What I know today is that the darkness has lifted, like the sea fog in Barmouth this morning. The landscape is no longer my foe, and the cold can be met head-on rather than shrunk back from. I don't care how stupid I look in my woolly hat as I clamber over the rocks towards a plunge pool. This is what I do. I plunge in, until the full force of winter assails my skin, the thermostat of cellular energy does its job as the dermal blood vessels constrict away from the surface, focusing on keeping the body core warm. Science goes so far, but my spirit will not be satisfied with these explanations. What the shock does is to wake me again and again – to living. All those months where I clung all day to the sofa, shuffled up to bed to switch on the TV at four and off again at ten and pill time, where 'MasterChef' and 'Ice Road Truckers', fake danger moments on television, distracted me from despair.

All that, and everything surrounding it is washed away by this cool concussion.

I holler with a fierce animal joy, dunk my shoulders and then spring out, my lungs momentarily forgetting how to draw breath. I am born again. I have gone into the dark, seen the empty rooms of my father and learned the hardest lesson he left for me. It's not always good to follow in your father's footsteps. In fact, fuck the mid-life crisis. There are jokes to make with my family, sandwiches to be wolfed and strong, sweet tea to revivify. Here is a day where we revisited the place of summer, wore its garland around our necks and gave thanks for the glad clarity of February water.

Lapwing, Venus Pool

River Clun, Beambridge

River Clun, Beambridge

WHEN THE BLUE LIGHT COMES and quilts the sky, the urge rises like sap. A river is a river whatever the season, and its call is the subtle song that drags me from my study, from my procrastinating perusal of that tax-avoiding purveyor of all things potential and possible called (with no irony) Amazon. A forest of consumables; indeed, their efficiency with delivery and returns almost evolutionary, the instant i-Click honing our species to expect quick-slick gratification. I tear myself away from this backlit box of delights-I-don't-need, vow to visit local shops, and go in search of coat and boots. The river-call is coming from Aston-on-Clun.

When the weather is like this, the car already warmed by the sun like a hand in a glove, I feel the need to hurry. If I don't get there fast enough, the moment will have clouded over, the sky have been stolen by all that is grey and godless. Up above my speeding vehicle, the crows are at their favourite pastime, harrying a lone red kite who shrugs off their black-shadowed efforts as she glides effortlessly against the singular blueness.

I park by the old industrial bridge that gives the few cottages comprising Beambridge its name. I have food, water, trunks and one of those ridiculously clever towels that packs up as small as a flannel, courtesy of the above-mentioned online emporium. A broken field gate leads into a footpath through a meadow that banks the River Clun. The intense saturation of colour above is reflected underfoot; the grass has taken on a new, verdant vibrancy. I walk down to the narrow river, scanning the trees for interesting bird life. The water is jewel-like. It catches the sun's rays and throws them back like tiny, tight javelins. It's a smile-blossoming sort of day.

Up above, in the bare-branched alders, I hear a thud of rhythmic hammering, but the woodpecker himself is elusive. I marvel at this ability of birds to fill denuded trees with sound and song, yet still to court invisibility. What I can see, though, as I peer fruitlessly into the branches, is the slow swelling of buds. They're getting ready to cancel the lie of winter.

I find the spot where I've spent many a 'working lunch' over the years. It's a small loop where the river almost curls around me. My jacket is discarded, swimming shorts pulled on and gentle steps taken over the sharp stones. It's still early enough in the year for the river not to be curtained off from my barefoot exploring by barbed ranks of nettles or the imported false pinks and whites of Himalayan balsam swaying like a mob of interlopers. The bank nearest to me contains a whole spread of died-back nettles, though they are already pushing forth tiny new leaves, eager to leave feet itchy and swollen. I have no choice but to work my way upstream. The mud I step onto looks solid enough but my foot sinks in above my ankle, as if the river would lure and cleave me to itself. The suck as I pull free is a sibilant groan. I tread much further out and paddle to a miniature pebble beach where I can study the Clun as she slips past.

What did the poet say, he who was not actually born a Shropshire Lad and who wrote many of the poems before he even set foot in the county, but who forged these hills and rivers into a landscape of lyrical imagination?

> In valleys of springs of rivers,
>
>> By Ony and Teme and Clun,
>
> The country for easy livers,
>
>> The quietest under the sun.

Here is quietness indeed and, while he may have used some geo-graphical licence in creating the landscape of the poems, the spirit of that melancholic man A.E. Housman watches over me, studying the ways of water. The surface tension is fascinating, like boiling gravy, this dimpling, this constant roiling burble, this shaking out of liquid sheets into ever shifting shape.

I'm delaying, the pause recalling memories of standing on the high point above the waterfall at Berriew, knowing that once I jump, I can't change gear and reverse. There will be shock, of course, the stealing of breath from lungs, as there always is, and the suddenness of the caught moment. Today, on this false spring morning before snow might return with the weight of Woe-Winter shouldering its way back into fields and gardens, my face warms in the sun. The river swirling past carries the cold current of months past. My feet are already numb, actually hurting with the chill – this is not Hampstead Ponds, with their city-induced warming, but the arctic breath of the high hills that lowers over the borders, the funnelling down of melted snow, the mingling of springs until even this mad March sun barely puckers the water's skin. However, it's not as though I haven't done this before. It merely *feels* like the first time, every time. I wade, fast – up to my waist, then dip down, in poor imitation of the swan as it searches out vegetation beneath the surface. I'm immersed, contained in this cold cauldron. *Like the first time, every time.* I'm in the river and the river's in me and the day is blessed.

I don't hang around, though. A few seconds' submersion is fine by me; I'm ready to get out. Let's be honest, there may even be some squealing as I flail back towards my towel; back into a sense of blood circulating as it's intended to and back to slower, regular breathing. As I shiver and dry off, the sound of a far-off tractor unexpectedly tenses me up. I dress fast, wondering at this feeling of unease. I sometimes get it when I stray, as I must admit I have done occasionally, from the starkly outlined footpaths, in search of the perfect swim. What is this flickering fear that makes me look in every direction? It is the sense of the illicit; each distant hum of a 4x4 fills with me a strange, sublime terror. What if I am caught and questioned? *Who are you? What are you doing here?* It happened once when I first moved to Shropshire and made the mistake of veering away from the OS map on one of the landed estates and encountered the great Master himself, owner of many farms and acres. He proceeded to ask my purpose, destination, address, even what I did for a living. I tried responding politely, in what I hoped was a friendly manner, and told him I was a poet. His eyebrows, honed through generations of gentry, rose high into his forehead and climbed even further when I asked him in turn what he did. His answer was like Alice's: 'Curious!', the single word slipping out crisply as he turned and abruptly stalked away.

Since then, I've remained nervous about the concept of privately owned land. Though, luckily, confrontations take place almost exclusively in my head, and perfect rebarbative answers about not owning the water in a bloody river come surging from my imagined lips. It's as if I believe I'm not allowed to feel this good, to actually let nature spill into me to wash away winter's dark, derogatory catcalls. As if the small doubts that I've stoked from embers through long grey afternoons really should ignite into flames. I am skiving, playing truant, unwilling to pick up emails, letting the apparatus of adulthood rust for a while as I go off gallivanting. I may be some time.

Even writing this begins to feel like shirking as ideas meander and loop. I allow the flow to pour onto the page, let each swim

Rooftop Swim, Icon Hotel, Hong Kong

DURING THE TWO DAYS before I leave for Hong Kong, my mind fills with the good old British combination of 'what can go wrong, will in fact do so,' alongside, 'I really don't deserve such fun.' But sod my negative interior voices. Sod the suburban sadness. I have a plane to catch.

I've come halfway across the world despite my mother's anxious concern that her boy – not long recovered from mental illness – would be possessed of such madness. However, this is the sanest of dreams and one I have nurtured since my teens. Having come close to the landscape of death, stood at its doors and inhaled its sickly, tempting incense, I have turned my face Janus-like in the other direction. I'm striding towards adventure, difference; less talk more action. I have, after all, created published worlds from the scratchpad of my mind, given them eco-systems, food, proverbs, religions. Now, it is the real world crooking an exotic finger to invite me in.

I search the internet obsessively before I leave, desperate to find the wild places even in such manufactured landscapes. Apparently, if I take rather a lot of buses and walk for hours into the wilderness, I *might* find the off-season waterfall and swimming hole. But when I arrive, Hong Kong is wreathed in smog, and sun is banished, so I feel less inclined to try.

Instead, I am in the city and I am pervaded by it. My days are short, under a week in total, and 'wild swimming' has transformed into a metaphor for urban navigation. It is the front crawl of culture, the dip and dive of food, smells and sights. However, for half my time here, I have made sure to book a hotel with a roof terrace pool that overlooks the harbour and the panorama of skyscrapers. As I

who a metaphor for urban city-dwellers in the front of the cityscape. For the dog and the lying faces, and so on. However, for half the time he's unlike sure to looked out on a cool temperate pool that might colour the earth and the partnership skyscrapers. As it

Hong Kong

confirmed to my somewhat jealous friends before I left, yes, I fully intend to have a proper James Bond pool experience.

First impressions are overwhelming. So many people, so many buildings crowding every street and encroaching on the clouds. Over seven million, with more arriving from China every day, are precariously squeezed onto land that is precious and thus expensive. If hills are too steep and jungly, and sea laps all around, the only answer is to build upwards. The Bank of China, its foundations surrounded by strange, immaculately landscaped fake waterfalls, is a case in point. This black edifice of odd, intrusive angles thrusting up into the sky has messed with the Feng Shui of all the other HK buildings it towers over. Of course, China now owns this island, so they can mess with it as much as they want, and if someone doesn't like it, well, it's not as if the Communist Party, frankly, my dear, gives a damn.

Water defines, sets boundaries, even invades the night-market on Yau Ma Tei. Among the array of restaurants, street stalls, outdoor sit-down places and holes in the wall, where laughter and gossip are served up alongside clams with chilli and garlic, there are shoals of shallow slopping plastic trays containing every kind of living fish. Once you make your choice, their contents turn to edible aquariums, truly the sea served on a platter. Shoe-horned among the leather fake-branded bags, smartphone covers, vegetable stalls and right next to the man repairing watches whose Rolexes are suspiciously cheap, is a brightly lit shop hung with dried fish and yellowing shark fins. The rest of the shark's body discarded, the fin often costs the equivalent of thousands of pounds and is served at wedding feasts to prove one's wealth and status. My stomach lurches. Great beasts dwindling to extinction for the satisfaction of show-offs.

My hosts for the first two days are Gert and Elizabeth, who belong to the voluntary organisation SERVAS. Its aim is simple, to promote peace through cultural exchange. Following several email conversations, my new hosts look after this just-joined member with a transparent goodness that washes away my disorientation while also overwhelming me with welcome.

One of the must-see, go-to spots is the fishing village of Tai O. After reading the literature about how *authentic* it is, I expect to be smacked round the face with a Disney-fied experience. I'm wrong, though. It is a village on stilts, properties squeezed into narrow strips and built out over the river banks with wooden pilings. There is a haphazard, rickety look about the place and the buildings succeed in defying gravity and perfecting the art of right angles. They are bodged together, a child's idea of houses scribbled chaotically, then covered in nailed-down sheets of tin to keep out rain and ward off typhoons. The river trip – right through the waterways that pass as streets – shows us houses backing onto the grey water, mothers putting out washing, families watching TV. This is no rehearsed show for the tourists. In amongst the teeming multiplicity, a white egret idly picks at the rubbish in the low-tide mud.

We step from the boat and soon become lost on wooden walkways that weave between houses like Ariadne's brittle thread. This is an urban minotaur's maze, suspended high above the river banks. The path grows narrower and narrower, passing homes that have collapsed in on themselves, and diving right through the middle of some dwellings where the locals – clearly well accustomed to us white 'gweilo' gawkers – carry on with the business of life. Once back on solid land, the narrow lanes exist only to create a shop front to almost every house – dried squid cooked on hot charcoal

43

grills, fresh egg waffles, wrapped in a cone to devour as you browse, green vegetables piled in sculptural cylinders, fish of every shape and size swimming in shallow, aerated trays. The tourists are like bees, sticking to the bright flowery lights of the main strip, but my ex-pat Afrikaans hosts know that wandering off the main path is the very essence of exploring. Their curiosity is rewarded as we turn a corner and find one of the few trees in the village, and a temple that looks more like a shed. No incense is burning this afternoon, but there is a quiet simplicity to the shrine, with its worn-away Buddha, whose face has been rubbed to a mask over hundreds of years. Nearby, men sit on a corner and chat, and a neon-lit kitchen reveals chairs and tables with raised edges where minutes before friends finished playing mahjong. That clack of shifting tiles is now silent as the dusk seeps in and we must find the last bus out of the village, to catch the late-night ferry over the waters back to Hong Kong Central.

The following night, I check into my hotel room and sit, just looking. I'm on the eleventh floor gazing out across the harbour at the asymmetric jumble of skylines where brands practise their free running in neon trainers that leap across the roofs of buildings. Moving adverts the size of cities. It all feels a bit sci-fi. Despite being force-fed this diet of corporate liquid light, somehow the evanescent blare of it, the vim and vigour of life and work and business here, fills me with a happy buzz – the honour of being witness to the miracle of remaking that is HK. Far below, dark waters slap against hidden piers, and at 8 p.m. precisely, green lasers cut the sky in a show that says to visitors and bored residents: this is HK, here I am.

I am also looking inwards at my ten-year-old self sitting on the iron radiator under the bay window of a dormitory at Belmont

School in 1975. The other boys, bullies by day with spit in their speech, and sarcasm furring their tongues, lay in bed, their cruelty softened by sleep. Here was my watching time, as the trees beyond and the lights of London below High Barnet spread before me, indicating the dream of more possibilities than the agony of school. Perhaps it was the promise of this sight now before me, braided out in silk and served with shrimp wonton. After the light show is finished, I take the lift down one floor, push open the glass door, and step out onto the wind-whipped roof terrace.

This is the moment for a broken boy made whole, when the glass-rimmed safety rail leads the eye out to the great harbour of Hong Kong, not hidden behind windows but there, blaring its neon pick-n-mix right into my star-struck eyes. It's even more impressive when the beamed-up night becomes the backdrop to my very wildest of swims. The pool is lit from within, all show, the stuff of movies. I dive in, greedy and glorious with the fact I have the whole pool and its wraparound terrace to myself. The water, with its sharp chlorine tang, is surprisingly cold. The breeze is strong enough to turn the pool into a seascape of tiny waves slapping at the side, spray hitting my face so that if I close my eyes, I could almost be back in the tidal grip of the Welsh waters of Barmouth. Though concrete and glass have managed to levitate my swim to ridiculous heights, they cannot banish nature.

I surface, continue my breast stroke, marvel to see for miles in every direction, as if I were the black kite itself, evolved inhabitant who soars by day in the canopy of this glass forest, mastering it for a moment, allowing its thermals, its secrets that funnel between apartment blocks, to blow and throw her in the endless freedom of updrafts. I am swimming, and flying, holding my hand out to the boy who was; saying, come with me, step out of the pettiness, april

Barmouth Lake

Small Lake near Cutiau, Barmouth

I HAVE HAD A BREAK, but my time away was surrounded on all sides by a winter that seemed to go on and on like some grey suburb with no greenery in sight. So I was surprised to hear that Barmouth had had a totally different experience. Here was where all the sunshine had decided to loiter, and snow had been allowed to dress only the highest peaks of Cadair Idris. True, all roads in and out were cut off, but Barbara who runs the antique shop on the High Street assured me that in the town, they had been snug as beaming bugs in rugs.

Today, the wind whips round the beach like a bossy horse rider, encouraging walkers and waves to go faster. We can see the sand eddying from a distance and have no wish for our ankles to be scoured. Inland is the better bet, so we pull on walking boots and stride out of town past Porkington Terrace and the temporarily closed Hotel Abermaw and on, up the steeply climbing road. The tarmac will peter out eventually, tall Welsh hills tend to have that effect, though not before it has wound towards Sylfaen Farm and the uplands. We'll be turning off long before then.

The lambs up here appear rather more relaxed than those at home in Shropshire, not having had to do battle with lethal snowdrifts. The tales from around the UK of frozen sheep mothers and their young were heartbreaking, even more for the farmers battling the free market of cheaply imported meat and the iron grip of the big four supermarkets. The extended winter has been a blow too much for too many and it is not surprising that the suicide rate among the farming community continues to be so high. Whenever I see Jenny from the next valley but one to ours, near Bishops Castle, I ask how her farm is doing. She reminds me every time that their sheep have long gone and her days of putting out the Texel ram to tup a flock of a hundred ewes are mere bleating memories.

Today, my twelve-year-old son is taking photos of little gangs of lambs – working out the possibilities of my new zoom lens, not listening to any words of fatherly camera advice from me. And I am hunting out other prey, hoping for the glitter of a reflection to catch my eye. Anticipation is a strange beast. We round a sharp bend and I'm suddenly convinced that the small lake I *know* should be right over there – with its spectacular view of Cadair mountain – has in fact dried up and been replaced by grass and heather. However, it's more likely that I'm somewhat geographically challenged and my condition is getting worse as I grow older. I'm developing a kind of geological dementia whereby valleys, lanes and hills appear before me that I'm certain were not there before, especially when I'm travelling at dusk and when the road is rendered unfamiliar and filled with shadows. Truly, journeys appear longer, and what lies around the corner is no longer assured.

But as we top the next rise, all is good and golden. The lake is before us and as inviting as cake. I have been reading Al Alvarez's *Pondlife*, a joyful hymn to ageing and the Hampstead Ponds he swims in on a daily basis. Whatever the season, he throws his body into temperatures down to the mid-thirties. He's definitely more the man than me, although my own winter dips elicit responses from both friends and strangers alike along the lines of 'complete nutter!' The strange irony is that, having been into more than one psychiatric unit in my life, wild water is often one of the few constant balms to my overloaded mind. Its shock value has fewer side effects than ECT (a treatment that has been mooted before for me, but which

I've so far avoided) and the calmness that descends after a wild swim knocks Valium off its frankly dangerous (for me) perch. As ongoing therapy, I recommend cold water.

I work my way round to the far side of the lake, battling with brambles that will make this way impassable by May. I find a natural green changing room, where the grass is soft and dry and the wind has flopped down like an exhausted toddler. Shorts on, towel hanging over a handy branch and I lever my way. On the other side, where the kids are sitting, watching, the reeds at the edge of the lake make for a mud broth of sinking squelch – a poor entrance into wide water. Over here, there is a natural vegetal shelf that takes the weight of my foot and bears it promisingly; a good platform from which to wade into deeper waters.

I hold up Alvarez today as my guru and ignore the cold clamping round my body as I shallow-dive forwards, swimming several strokes before I realise quite how much of winter has been stored in this lake; the very opposite of a night storage heater. It's a brief swim, but a swim nonetheless. My body is burning and I yelp melodramatically for my audience of three as I thrash back to shore, back to the glow of it all and the goodness of life. And like the addict I am, as soon as the blood begins to flow once more, I plunge back in for a second go. As my son used to say when he was little and I would lie down and balance him on my shins and raise him high up into the air, 'Again! Again! Again!'

There are so many small joys in this world and this is one of them. The whole of me trembles, is suffused with interior warmth. I imagine I could open my mouth and sing the very kites from the sky to come and land on my outstretched arms. Perhaps this is an intimation of what it is like to ride the thermals on the blue days, wings outstretched, quartering the land for rabbit or vole, where

52

the air is the element of soaring – it is your road, your neighbour-hood and every current and updraft is a known intimacy. Would that I could take the photo that would catch Buzzard, Kite or Peregrine in flight-spread sharpness rather than a distant smudge of feather and claw.

Soon I am dressed and am filled to the brim with goodwill; all of life's rattiness and fear has been chucked back in its proper place. My daughter and son wave and shout for me to get a move on. They remind me that there is apple crumble in the fridge and custard to heat up when we return, and they'd like that to be quite soon please. In fact, they yell, waving again, they'll make a head start. I'm up for that. I'm up for all of it.

Red kite, More

may

The village of 'anonymous'

A Trail of Open Gardens and a River

MAY, A MONTH OFTEN STUFFED with posters and leaflets for village 'Open Gardens'. Curiosity, inspiration and sheer nosiness is a great motivator to get me out of the house and up into the hills. There's a back route to the tiny hamlet I'm heading for, situated over the high ridgeways above one of the historic market towns. I use an old-fashioned guidance system that doesn't recalculate to avoid traffic jams, or choose the main road rather than the meandering B-route that takes longer, but which gives out views for free. My Philips 1.7 miles-to-the-inch, large-format map book has saved me many times over the years. Now, in this borderland where mobile and satellite signal vanish into the clefts and shadowed hills, it is my only old-school choice. My finger traces out roads where grass and moss have invaded the tarmac, carving out a thin eco-system in the centre of what is really little more than a farmer's track. We meet no cars, no walkers, and once we have left the valley behind, above are only the ever-present kite and buzzard. (Ever-present that is until the exact moment I whip out my camera lens. 'Now you see us…now you…ha-ha, sucker!')

Tucked into my camera backpack are my trusty trunks and micro towel; a village near my destination straddles a river and I can scent the possibility of a swim. First, though, there's art to be savoured at an exhibition in a village hall and gardens to be walked round.

There is something reassuring about the institution of Open Gardens. Out there in the big world, the US is trying to catch Edward Snowden, the man who told us that this so-called democracy and champion of human rights has in fact been spying, listening and tapping into our every move. On other pages of the papers are details of wars and deaths and crashes and yet more cuts.

But still, here in the green-fingered realm of Open Gardens we sow seeds, pull weeds, cut the borders of our lawns and make beauty out of wildness, then sit on folding chairs and chat to a steady stream of visitors. It is delightful, hopeful, an afternoon filled with colour and scent, everything growing and blooming and all seeming creatively possible.

In the local church, there is a display of book art, where form and function meet text in most surprising ways. Books become sculpture, home of fold-out accordion stories, flip books, cylinders, boxes, pop-ups, origami, cut-outs. I love the idea of the familiar landscape occupied by printed/written words being deconstructed, the materiality forging something new. The poet and sculptor Miriam Obrey has a poem spread with artwork over ten sheets, about the famous gargoyles at Kilpeck Church in Herefordshire. Her poetry is lyrical, bringing these stone uglies to life, 'Clawfooted slapheads with trunks and tumbrels/Dripstones and Crick-necks, with mossy fingers...', imagining them 'kettled' on the roof. It is a great treat to enjoy such crafted writing.

Two days ago, I made an author visit to a secondary school in Worcester. I asked the Year Eight teenagers how many of them read books. The show of hands was as sparse as the hair on most newborns. After twenty-five years of visiting schools I'm seeing the evidence of changing times. All too often, sustained curiosity, thirst for immersion in the new, the unknown are sacrificed at the altar of all that is internet and instant and free. The World Wide Web is perhaps our modern version of Yggdrasil, the Tree of Knowledge. And knowledge can be a wonderful thing. Dictators uncovered, truths ferreted out, scholarship shared. But on YouTube one can find farting donkeys, and horrible skateboard accidents in full and gory detail. And there are TV shows for people who really, really 'want it', who 'only have to dream hard enough' without working solidly on learning the craft of whatever talent they were born with; so many who appear to believe it is their human right to 'be the one'. So, hey, why waste time with words on a page when you can't even 'like it' or see if it is 'trending'?

It's no surprise that I linger over all the pieces of book art today, that I delight in their veracity. These are all works by local artists who have poured their craft and heart into forms and pages that physically come to life, creating tiny performances, diminutive stage sets.

As the afternoon wears on, I'm filling up with views and inventive planting and chats (with owner/gardeners and fellow visitors) and photos and bench-lingering and the warmth of human contact. I've even managed to cadge a guided tour of a fantastic barn conversion, so now I can add envy to the list.

I see a friend who leads the singing group I'm part of. Over the years we've sung in churches, by rivers and inside stone circles, adding our voices to those of the rising skylarks. She lives in another village nearby and, what's more, oh joy, knows the local swimming spot I was hoping to sniff out. Curiosity is both driver and giver of small but bountiful secrets. Over the years and all over the UK, I've asked local people where the known swimming holes are – if there are any – and I've then promptly leavened work trips with a dip and delve.

I follow the verbal directions I've been given and find the right path, secure in my friend's information that the farmer whose land borders the river is pretty tolerant of considerate dippers and only likely to get irate if there's a crowd intent on drunkenness or generally unpleasant behaviour. As there is only one of me and my last drink was in 1984, I think I'll fit quite neatly into the landscape. A green lane leads off the hill and down into the valley, where a meadow of buttercups and high grasses strives to hide the river beyond. By a somewhat ramshackle cattle bridge, I pick my way through nettles to a pebble beach. I'm hot, I'm sweaty and I'm anxious for water, swatting at the persistence of horseflies.

Though the village lies a mere hundred or so yards away, I'm totally alone. There is only the river and me. This late in May, the water no longer carries the sharp breath of earlier months and the jolt of cold is more of a gentle buzz. I can wade, in an almost leisurely fashion, to find the deepest scooped-out pool beneath the bridge and dunk myself slowly under. It is entirely good and full of grace to be alive here. I never tire of the repetition, do not generally think how much better it would be in the Bahamas. For the grass is greener right in front of me, by the banks of this supple river. I'm many miles upstream from Ludlow, where the river is a great, silty presence whose depths are invisible. Up this high, at one of the many criss-cross spots where England and Wales can't quite determine which side of the border they are standing on, the river is more of a runnel, a shallow song that hollows and carves out occasional pools.

Downstream, just beyond the bridge, a bird accelerates along the bank, then swerves to land on an island with a flourish. My first thought, given its speed, is: kingfisher? But the colour is wrong, too much brown. Then I see its tail begin to bob up and down and I think, ah, here is the emblem of what I do, bobbing round these local rivers. For we are both visitors, comfortable by water, in fact unable to do without it. I salute my fellow dipper and head off in search of homemade scones with cream and local raspberry jam and a cup of good old WI tea. However many services the current government seeks to cut, however many libraries and community arts initiatives and rural bus schemes are closed down, the river, the water, that bobbing bird unbothered by the gawky guy upstream will still be here, still celebrating the flowing dreamlines of Britain that brought me here today. There's a constancy to water, when all around is cruel change and uncertainty.

Postscript: I wrote the first draft of this chapter while drinking my tea back in the local village hall. I was so enamoured of this place and of this beautifully orchestrated event that I returned with the whole family the following day. The sky continued to hold up a canopy of ridiculous blue and my son and I both braved the cool pool under the bridge. I saw my singing friend again and asked her to read the chapter. She enjoyed it but was wary of the village's secret swimming point actually being named (as it was in that draft). Further downstream, she told me, a swim-hole that had become well known was often overrun with thoughtless, loud, rubbish-strewing day- or night-trippers, many more intent on getting spirits down their necks than seeing the spirit of the land slap bang in front of them. Hence the tacit 'respectful locals only' at play in her own village dunking spot. It's a delicate balance between landowners and would-be walkers and dippers like me and it's one I try to be mindful of.

I've already mentioned the estate in our village where locals are able to walk and to ramble the length of the lakes. It is a relaxed and generous stance on the part of the owners, though no one with any sense would take advantage of it or invade their privacy.

Elsewhere in these pages, I have felt and do feel ambivalent about land, and rights to access water. The encounters I've had have veered from outright warmth and friendliness to peremptory, haughty challenges. But in this case, I understand the need for anonymity. Let it rest in my memory and in the folds of itself.

Canada geese, Dolydd Hafren

june

Shelve Pool and Cordon Hill from the Stiperstones

Shelve Pool, Stiperstones

I AM IN SEARCH OF WILD WATER. On hot days, I cleave to it like the fluttering moth to the lure of lamplight. As a full-time writer, words can only take me so far. And when the head is throbbing and my wrists ache with the constant click of the keyboard, I have to surrender. I must give in to the urge, slip into my car and find those out-of-the-way places where I can lose myself in all that the borderlands have to offer. I don't rely on weather forecasts, only casting my eye up to the sky, the bluer the better.

On this particular June afternoon, I have in mind a pool in the valley beneath the hamlet of Shelve. My windows are wound down as I thread past the abandoned mine shafts and complexes where lead and barytes were once hauled from the earth. Fingers of brick and stone are all that's left here of Shropshire's industrial past. Where great oak engine wheels turned, today birds perch. I try to imagine all that noise, all the bustle of business. The hills are filled with hollowed-out chapels, their prayers the bleating of sheep passing through, their once-vaulted roofs now the thinnest of blue skies.

At the edge of the woods, I park and cross the road to the footpath that leads me straight through a farmyard, with no indicator of the delights that lie beyond.

It's a proper June day, the sort we dream of in January, so I'm wearing only shorts, sandals and T-shirt. I walk fast, determined to work up a sweat, and I savour the strange anticipation running through my veins like wild briar.

I don't move so quickly that I can't stop and marvel, though – at the persistence of life. Out of the top of a weather-worn fencepost, a small ash sapling bravely climbs towards the sun.

From wood, grows wood. Truly, it's a topsy-treevy world. The underside of my day has included a ridiculously bulging inbox, the frustrations of edits and redrafts, and a daunting 'to do' list. So this small sign of life's vitality makes me smile.

I follow the footpath, skirting the hilly curves of pastureland and soaking up far views of Corndon Hill, before dipping down though lush grass that strokes my ankles. The pool itself is well disguised with a belt of silver birch, alder and tall rushes topped by slender black cylinders that resemble dark altar candles. This seems appropriate, for I am seeking my own kind of mass, a liturgy of landscape that intones to me and beckons me on. The footpath skirts round the pool's far edges until at last a liquid flatness spreading for at least a hundred yards is revealed.

Once more I realise why I was lucky to marry a Shropshire lass. How can I imagine living anywhere else? The valley, the pool, the hills around are utterly empty, apart from a couple of irritable-looking crows with nothing to harry. The crows cough, though not politely, and disappear behind the trees.

If you could put in an advance order for the perfect day for a dip, this is it. The heat is just right, all of June contained in it and the promise of more summer to come. I get changed, but keep my sandals on to splash over the rocky sub-surface at the near bank. Rushes stand and lean to my right. Mallards squawk on my left, pretending affront at my daring to slip into their space. The water is dark, not choosing to reveal its secrets. And it's so cold that it burns. My trick today is to not hesitate. With a head-forward immersion, I strike out and away from the comfort of the shore. Slow breast stroke is the best method. I'm not here to race, but to see where I'm going.

When there is only the weight of the water to buoy you up

and you are fifty yards out, treading the depths – that is the moment. If you sank, no one would know. But as I let go of vague ancestral fears of lurking beasts ready to bite me in two, another feeling wraps round my now glowing body. It's the response I've described for each dip. Alive! Alive! Alive! Nothing pins me so firmly in the moment as this. Right now, as my arms and legs turn slowly to keep me suspended. Right now as, in the distance, the great quartzite outcrops of the Stiperstones etch the jagged horizon, reminding me that they are some of the oldest rocks in this world, having stood sentinel for four hundred and eighty million years. Their jaggedness is the gift of the Ice-Age glaciers they looked down on. The constant thawing and re-freezing shattered the quartzite into the scree that is the bane of walkers and fragile ankles these days.

I turn and float and into my mind pours one of the many stories of Wild Edric of the Borderlands. A version of his tale has him fast asleep, with his slumbering huntsmen by his side, deep under the very hills above me today. Sleeping for many hundreds of years, he wakes and rides out when Britain has need of great warning. So it is told that his shrill hunting horn was heard and that he and his men were seen riding wildly in the months before the Crimean War and again before WW1. I wonder when he might come to warn us again? Will the madness of our destruction of the natural world, the accelerating extinction of our animals, the pouring of plastic into our seas finally stir him from his sleep? I certainly hope so.

Right now my limbs are warning me of the distance back to shore. A heavy sluggishness has set in and even doggy paddle seems like a lot of effort to keep propelling me all the way to shallow safety. My feet are a purplish blue when they finally scrabble over slippery rocks onto dry grass and I flop down in the warmth, grasping at breath. I can't even feel my fingers but I have a strong remedy in my bag: sweet, milky coffee. I may have slid surreptitiously from my study earlier, but not before passing through the kitchen to nab the essentials – food and a full thermos. It's still scalding hot and while the caffeine works wonders inside, the heat of the cup thaws my fingers. Of course, everything tastes better after a wild swim; more intense, and today is no exception. My sandwiches are crammed with a creamy, locally made cheese called 'The Cheese With No Name'. And, though it may be travelling incognito, with a false beard and moustache, it's a cheese to put fuel and fire back where they belong.

I pack everything carefully and roll up a little bit of Shelve Pool to carry away with me: the tang of lake-water on my skin, the memory of it in the smile that hovers like a dragonfly, the cold of it recharging me as I go back to work and to everyday chores – picking up kids, cooking dinner, tidying up. All the cutlery of daily life has been given an extra shine by my small adventure, my half-hour dip in the middle of the day.

River Teme, Bromfield, Earl of Plymouth Estates

MY DAUGHTER, ROZ, AND I have been studying the muggy greyness that is a disappointing substitute for sky, convinced that a local but new-to-us wild swimming hole has to be out there, to be jumped in today. The website wildswimming. co.uk is regarded as something of a fount of all knowledge when it comes to all subjects outdoor and watery that don't include chlorinated swimming pools. Shropshire features only sparingly and, I have to admit, that's the way I like it. Over years that turned

River Teme, Bromfield

to decades, I have generally been the only water dipper at most places I visit.

I recall one of the Shropshire references on the website, decide to head out to it and grab my wild swimmer's book and necessaries. On the way, we stock up at the Ludlow Food Hall – of course, no swim without treats straight after. We buy enough for a picnic. But when we get back in the car I realise that Daniel Start's excellent *Wild Swimming* book doesn't contain the information for our destination; his website was my source. This being Shropshire, the mobile signal is rubbish and my phone refuses to load either internet or maps. I only remember the name of the village itself – Bromfield – but as we're nearly there anyway we set off hopefully, for a trip that lasts all of three hundred yards until a pull-in by the church. We park and walk down to the river and the old abandoned mill, now slowly being restored.

By the bridge over the Teme, it's with relief that Roz spots the footpath sign tucked down by the stonework. Like me, she can feel nervous when crossing private land, even when legal and clearly marked. I too get rattled, but for different reasons. It's that sense of nature being owned lock stock and barrel, of privileged rights over swathes of wild water which brings back the ghosts of the poet John Clare and historic Enclosure when much common land was partitioned and ancient rights of foraging and grazing stolen.

So we are both reassured by the large sign here marking a choice of walking directions. The route splits: left towards Ludlow or right upstream. Suddenly, the grey day, thick with heavy humidity that presses down positive thought, begins to brighten up. We wander for a while and then pick our way through docks and nettles, looking for a shallow beach where we can set up camp and from where I can launch myself. Ahead of us, almost hidden in the weeds, a man in a flat cap appears to be rooting around. I wonder if he is a birder or just an old country lad looking for wildlife. We skirt past him and find a nettle-beaten track towards the river, with a perfect beach of smooth round pebbles.

However, I am aware of the chap a little further back, wondering what he's up to, wondering if perhaps he's the Earl of Plymouth himself on whose land these footpaths traipse. As I am getting changed, we hear crunching footsteps and there he is, striding right down onto our little beach. Old fears surface. I turn and strike up what I hope is a cheery and civil conversation opener. I ask if he's searching for fish. He responds in a clipped tone, 'This is totally private fishing here.'

Ah! Is that why he's checking us out? I gesture to my small bag and assure him that we're here only for a picnic and a bit of a swim.

He nods, silently, and gazes across the river. On the bank opposite, a small, dark green rowing boat is lurking. We all contemplate it and he tells us it shouldn't be over there. Clearly some local lads have 'borrowed' it for teenage jinks. This is what he's been looking for, as it's the boat used by the keeper, from which he cuts low-lying branches and keeps the river clear for the fishermen. Basic river clutter-clearance. He mutters to himself that now he will have to get round to the opposite bank to move the boat. I am in my swimming trunks already and it strikes me that it would really be no big deal to wade over and drag back the boat. I suggest it. It's one of those moments when an encounter turns.

The look on his face as I push across, untie the boat and haul it in, is one of surprise and unexpected pleasure. I have turned into the kind stranger, albeit somewhat bonkers to be swimming.

Suddenly, as I hand over the rope, he becomes voluble. We talk and I tell him that I'm an author working on a book about wild swimming, and hoping my daughter can take some good photos of me in the water. He shivers and informs me that some of what now swirls around my ankles in mid-June is still Welsh mountain meltwater, the snow and ice of winter mellowed but thrumming with the bite of another season as it slows its way through Shropshire.

I discover that this well-spoken, old-fashioned gentleman is not, in fact, the Earl of Plymouth, but the Estate Manager, Barry Jenkins. I am curious, humble and very happy to learn from his flowing expertise on this stretch of the Teme. He points out different types of mayfly and tells how the rise in the cormorant population has decimated smaller fish stocks. However, he relates that there are now larger trout than ever on this stretch, with salmon still reaching the high teens in pounds. Then there are other tales, confirmed by my own memories of the local rivers. Far more silt is washing down into the water, and pebble beaches that once had clean, smooth stones are now coated, as if the whole bed of the river had turned a dull beige. The water shrimp, freshwater mussels and local populations of crayfish have vanished, thanks unhappily to God knows what concoction of chemicals we humans are happy to let sluice from farm and factory into our rivers.

We both shrug our shoulders, unsure of reasons. and I ask if it's OK for me to carry on swimming. He's more than happy in this particular instance. He thanks me again for my help with the boat, expresses hope that his wife might grill him a trout for lunch and he wishes me good luck with the book before ambling off through the fields. Of such meandering meetings is life made.

To swim where one is allowed feels delicious and oddly grown up. I have a right to this river, can glide slowly without fear of discovery, sharing space with hopping pond skaters and ever-present swarms of river flies. I feel as leisurely as the Teme itself, no longer swollen with floodwater. The pace is gentle, a long man drifting in a green-leaved tunnel. I swim, and Roz snaps away. Afterwards we eat our lunch in that calm stony glade, under the dappled shade of alders, the breeze off the water dispelling the mugginess of June. We are hopeful of but never actually see the kingfishers that patrol this stretch. Lunch safely digested, a post-picnic quick dip seems compulsory. Then, we make another gruelling three-hundred-yard drive back to the Ludlow Food Hall Café, where most of the food comes from the estate we have been exploring, and where a flat white coffee fuels the tapping of my fingers and sharpens the memories of my swim. I find later that the spot we discovered was entirely different from the one located on the website. So, after all, there is something to be said for the memory lapse and misremembering of middle age that led us to this place.

River Lugg, Aymestrey

WHAT IS THIS HEAT that beats down on the windows and walls of our stone chapel? Already, the blinds are drawn in my study, but the light leaks in, and with it comes a promise. The bright kingdom of outdoors is waiting, if only I can put work and the weight of everything else to one side for a few hours. When will such days come again? June has properly arrived, triumphantly dressed in the folds of blue reminiscent of those the painters of Bruges crushed from lapis lazuli some seven hundred years ago.

River Lugg, Aymestrey

From a recent weekend away, we have garnered goodies from the stalls set up in Bruges Market Square, under the great tower of commerce that lowers over what was once the world's first stock exchange. We still have fresh herb-covered goat's cheese and thin slices of smoked ham. There were many stalls stuffed into the huge square, the best easily indicated by long queues of locals. A few days later, and this little bit of Bruges is picnic-ready to come along for the ride to one of our favourite places.

Roz is on exam-leave, and her days are full of Russian history and Stalin's talents in the starvation of millions. The irony is not lost on us. The car is already toasted and the seats sticky with heat as we wend our way from Shropshire to the Herefordshire borders. We were introduced to this spot by our friend Emma fifteen years ago. She lived in a cottage near the banks of the River Lugg, and was keen to share this glorious swimming hole. We have returned many, many times since.

We swoop through the green lanes, dip and soar like diesel swallows, finally turning off the A-road that courses through Leintwardine and Wigmore, before we dive down a tiny lane near Aymestrey. Instantly, the road narrows and the trees stretch overhead until we are canopied in dimpled shadow. In the steep, vertiginous woods to our right there are deer, shy shade-dwellers, their ability to vanish enough to make spies jealous. We park by an old weir gate, part of the huge infrastructure that once covered the valley and which no doubt powered the now long-silent mills. These days, the gate's only purpose is to provide a narrow bridge to cross.

Winter was cruel here. It re-rendered the course of the river, gouged new banks, took old beaches and certainties away. That, and the spring floods which, when last I visited, had turned all defined features into a bright brown surge that no wild swimmer would be insane enough to risk. Today, calmness has returned. A fallen tree trunk straddles the middle of the weir, a few strands of Himalayan balsam already sprouting from the mossy wood. Out of death, life. The pebble beach on which we usually spread out is under dense leaf, too shadow-chilled. Instead, we barefoot it across the lip of the weir, treading on the soft, underwater mossy-stuff that is velvet underfoot. A meadow spreads on the other side, an intense green saturation. Roz and Polly take to the sun. I turn to the water.

At the top of the weir, part of a sluice gate has been repaired. It makes a perfect diving platform and, for a while, I teeter on the edge of it, wondering if by chance sharp, strange things, washed down by seasonal storms, are waiting in the murk. These are the beasts that glide in the rivers of our dreams. Yet, while it is of course always wise to check out any possible unseen risks below the surface, I know this stretch well. It's deep and there's nowhere for large stuff to catch. So there is only the now-or-never moment left, the one where I am warm and the sun is on my back like a friend and I know that in seconds I shall be shivering, grasping for the shore at the shock of it.

I leap, savour the split second of flight, of defying gravity, then strike the surface and plummet through, unlike any water boatman insect. A friend who knows about my wild-swimming addiction once compared my immersions to a kind of self-flagellation. My wife Polly laughed! But I wouldn't do it unless there was gain and glow. For whatever lethargy, anxiety, work worry, or future fear carouses around my head, in that instant of arriving in the water, it is gone, slam-splash-dunked. Again, I return to that natural lyricist Richard Jefferies, who wrote: 'There was delight in the moment, but it was not enough. I swam, and what is more delicious than swimming? It is exercise and luxury at once.'

As I surface and gasp, there is only fierce joy. I clamber out onto the bank, shake myself like a Labrador, feel the tingle on my skin, in my heart, my thoughts – turn round and jump in again ...then again.

The magic of the valley unfolds. Beyond the gentle twists and turns of the river, a single house looks down from a far hill. Like following a ritual, a catechism, when I stand here gazing, I often place myself on that far veranda on some summer's evening, looking out at all this nature, knowing that despite the darkness the daily news is so keen for us to imbibe, there is goodness and beauty and striving. That distant house, the occupation of which I've made in my mind, becomes the monk's cell, the Buddhist sanctuary, the place of meditation and possibility. It's time to leave. The cows drift away from me as I return through thick grassy meadows.

Back by the weir, Polly and Roz are both reading. I dress and stroll along the edges of meadows, inadvertently disturb the lazy lambs and sheep in a shady copse, and arrive at a far bend in the river where no house can be seen, no lane, no path, no people. Only woods, grass, the soft whir of dragonfly. The loop of water here is pregnant-bellied, serene. I didn't bring my towel, but that doesn't prevent me from enjoying my second swim and my first skinny-dip of the year.

What would I look like, a naked beanpole, wearing water sandals! Who cares? The gently shelving mud leads into cool depths and I swim slowly, through water turned brighter by the clearness of sky. For these moments everything else recedes again: work worries, money, growing old, the fear of depression returning – in fact the latter becomes utterly impossible when immersed in the joy of this clean water, this valley and the blessings of family. And it's a feeling only reinforced on my way back by the vivid and jewelled green brooches of damselflies adorning the nettles and posing for my camera.

Later, after we've packed up and the Lugg is behind us, a memory rises of a dark November dusk, when I was on my way to mid Wales to present and film a TV programme about drovers' roads for a series rightly called 'Heart of the Country'. It is strange to think of those other pathways through the land, where cattle and sheep were walked great distances on foot. Those ancient tracks faded into history once trucks became the acceptable way of moving livestock to their market destination, leaving only milestones and trodden ways where grass still grows shorter centuries later. That late afternoon, fifteen years ago, a younger me, full of ambition and goals, stopped here, crazy with river lust, and swept the evidence of seasons aside. I could hardly see the water, as if the landscape was melting into dark under my feet. But still I waded in and submerged myself in that breath-thievery of cold, in the dare of it, in the loneliness of the place where summer was only a similarity of outlines: this stone wall, that sluice gate, that familiar path where nettles are merely ghosts.

Like a walker beating the bounds to confirm his parish, I've ducked, dunked and swum here year round, my body a pendulum of all weathers, ticking and marking temperature changes in the spirit's relentless urge. The memory of that chill night slips away and we drive home under the blue-beaten rim of sky, filled to the brim with this day.

River Clun, Clun Castle

THE SKY HAS BEEN SMUDGED this last week, a bleary hangover of cloud-blur. It is only suited to moody photographs and digital manipulation applied from the warmth of my study. I've been adding the glow of Lightroom, tweaking colour back into the washout of outdoor images. So, when a day that is different from the preceding greyness awakens and crooks its finger, it's just as well to take heed and take heart. This morning, I've been about the business of garden tidying, attacking the hedges and giving thanks for the technology of lithium ion batteries as they power my cordless cutter. I'm hot and sweaty. The antidote is obvious.

There are some mornings that I wake up with an instinctive knowledge of the exact spot I will swim that day. I can lie awake with it, floating belly-up with insouciance, a wavering mirage that it is my task to make real. So, weekend duties done, children dealt with, lawn looking shocked and embarrassed as a shorn lamb, I slip away through the valleys towards Clun. When I reach the edges of this small town, my heart rises. The place is buzzing today. Outside the café, there must be at least two holiday-makers sipping tea, and when I reach the small car park next to the river, I count four other cars. I wonder if we can cope with such an influx! Thanks be to the avatars of greenery, of houses settling comfortably into the armchair of valley and hill, a little worn and frayed at the edges. Perfect. There is still the higgledy-piggledy, the piecemeal adding-on of centuries that layers the land, and is an affront to the development of the last fifty years, during which houses were magicked into boxes, great stunted blocks of them, squeezed into lidded cul-de-sacs, shut tight against community and communication. Not here, though.

Once I have everything I need in my camera bag, I set off over the footbridge towards the castle. The huge, irregular hillock that rises before me was deposited in the last Ice Age, a gift of glaciers long melted into oceans. Crouched on top lie the ruins of another age. A hill was easy to defend, so build, ye English, but beware, for the Welsh, with good reason and too many taxes, were angry. The earlier wooden castle was burnt once by Prince Rhys, and again eighteen years later by Prince Llewellyn ap Lorwerth. Later, again, for war is forever repetitive, the whole town was razed to the ground when the new stone battlement proved impregnable. I read this information on the same day that, in Syria 2013, the army of Assad have retaken the strategic town of Qusair. Footage showed the spoils were thin – charred concrete, buildings reduced through the instant entropy of bombs into rubble. At its heart, a pockmarked central tower containing a broken clock and the newly raised flag of the military. The king is dead, long live the king. The populace have fled. There is no town of Qusair any more.

I feel sobered and find it difficult to shake the images and news from my head. Yet as I stand high on the castle mound looking along the valley to Newcastle-on-Clun and the aptly named Far Forest, all the machinations of men fade slightly and become distant. Nature has crept back up and over the ruined remains here. It has become a sensitively managed balance of preservation and wild wreck, courtesy of English Heritage. Where once might have been expensive glass, or simple wooden shutters, now only air cradles the hills beyond. There is nothing left to defend, no principality to lord over. It's a seat of long lost power, but still imposing for all its reduction. It's also rather photogenic and happy to be caught in bracketed exposures. If I play my technique

River Clun, Clun Castle

right – one dark, one just right, one way too light – I can combine my shots to stretch the eye into the furthest reaches of dynamic range, like a magician pulling off an awesome reveal. Here is the window frame, no longer in shadow, and the furthest view behind, perfectly lit, every detail illuminated as a book of hours! *Voilà!*

Sometimes I watch the yearning of photographers to fill their shots with glow, to add effect, and I see a deeper desire to express the very this-ness of all that lies around us. Perhaps it's something of a spiritual echo, though I'm certain that cynics would snub their noses at such a notion. But really, when I tweak out the green in a shot, or turn the sky a darker blue to wow the viewers on Flickr, I do think I'm maybe trying to reach back, and back further yet again towards an Eden.

Today, there's no need of that; photography is my addendum, the river is where it's at. There is a particular area in an overgrown meadow below the castle, filled with dandelion, buttercup and nettle. Here, the river finds a corner and bends accordingly, wrapping round the base of the castle like a flowing moat. I pick my way down the steep path and lay out my towel. A pair of orange-tip butterflies dandle about the overgrowth, semaphoring the fact that it really, truly is summer.

Polly and I found this corner of the River Clun in summer 1991 when we were just married and had moved to Shropshire from Bristol. So it has been the scene of picnics for two, then three, then four, besides stone-skimming sessions, dive-bombing, tiny wellies paddling, boat-floating, dam-building and minnow-chasing. It's a small curve that contains our past and our present and many of our golden days. I'm not sure when we stopped scraping together dam fortifications with pebbles, mud and grass, or how we found ourselves with our oldest at Sixth Form and our youngest at secondary school, but I do feel nostalgic for two childhoods vanishing into the depths like elusive trout.

The thing about a river is that you always have to come back to the present. Though I'm treading on Victorian and early twentieth-century shards of pottery, and even older glacial pebbles – and what lies beneath my feet is not really the land of this precise geographical location, but the run-off from distant fields and the mobility of rain – yet, there is only one moment I can dive into: and it is this one. You would think by June that British rivers might finally admit, publicly, that really, yes really, it *should* be a bit warmer. But no. The chill beneath the serried banks of alders is enough to make me strike ridiculous Iron-Man poses in sheer shock. However, it doesn't take long to acclimatise and I breast-stroke upstream, keeping my mouth firmly closed to avoid the airborne midges. The swifts, as they swing through impossible orbits, are welcome to the insect feast. Fast food, literally.

The verb 'swim' may be a slight exaggeration of what is possible, as there are really only around ten yards or so of available swimming before the water turns to shallows once again. Yet it is – and always has been – enough, this wallowing under the ruins, gliding back and forth in the deep shade. The alder trees are unkempt, branch-strewn, unused shadows of their former selves. My friend Rob, who has lived here all his life, tells me that Clun was once at the heart of the clog-making industry. Each winter, itinerant labourers would camp out in this cold frost-bowl of a valley and coppice the alders for their wooden crop. Roughed-out clog soles were stacked to dry by the banks of the Clun, in circles ten foot high and four foot across. When Rob was a boy, an old road-mender from up at Twitchen told him of a great flood that happened when he was a child. I pause to work out the maths.

Rob is in his fifties, so was probably told this story back in the 1960s/70s. If the man was old then, we have drifted all the way to the early 1900s, before the Great War. Different times, when the whole valley vanished in a great shining lake, and the clogs floated off downstream. The local children were paid to recover them – a penny for ten. An old Shropshire lad tells a story and it too floats downriver to me.

I am the only one here now on this warm Sunday in a landscape once known as the 'honour of Clun'. Well, I am happy to honour this flow from past into present. The meadow is empty and I see no one apart from a pair of knees high up on the skyline of the castle, indicating a snoozing visitor, soaking up the vibes of history. The long grass is bursting with dandelion lamps and if I were to kneel, to blow, to wish, then these clocks might split apart, unwind and whir like little white pendulums, marking these delightful stretched-out June days.

july

Ludlow Weir

Ludlow Weir, River Teme

I STAND ON THE LIP OF LUDLOW WEIR, water bursting over the edge and furring my feet with its brown coldness. I'm poised to dive, clothes piled on the gnarled concrete bank behind me, near to where a group of teenagers are already tucking into cans of cider with percentages designed by manufacturers to help the imbiber work out how fast they can get pissed. I'm hoping they don't nick my stuff. However, they seem intrigued by the middle-aged beanpole in trunks, preparing to embark on a curious activity: swimming, in a river.

Fraught with delicious anticipation and pestered by the sensible monkey who whispers in my ear that what I am about to do is barmy, I dawdle. The moment reminds me of standing on a similar lip, in the middle of a Leicester industrial estate not so many years ago. It was the top of a vertical ramp about thirteen feet high, the curve of it edged by a scratched metal rail, and my mode of transport was a skateboard. Not the tiny modern boards no bigger than Pop-Tarts favoured by teenagers, but a proper, full-blown deck for grown-ups, with fast wheels and even faster bearings. I was forty-three and I *knew* I was either about to hurt (a lot), break something or live. I stood with my right foot on the tail of the board wedged over the edge. All I had to do was press down hard and quick with my left, front foot and gravity would do the rest. A proper mid-life crisis. And I wasn't the only one. We even had an online forum – middle-age-shred.com. All those guys and girls from the Seventies who had been there at the beginning of skating and had worked out recently that they weren't getting any younger, life was too short, etcetera. Surprising fun was to be had, adrenaline to be tasted. We'd hire out skate parks for a night and hit the north: Blackpool, Wigan, Bolton and Burnley where indoor wooden ramps resounded to the rush of polyurethane.

Now, as then, I had an audience of teenagers. That lot were perhaps rather keen to see me bail. YouTube is full of accidents with millions of hits. I prayed to the gods of speed and leaned forward with all my weight. In the rush that followed as I fell, then accelerated out of the curve and onto the flat, I forgot to breathe. The teenagers burst into applause. An old man dropping vert. What a sight!

Those years have gone; my second adolescence packed away in the garden shed along with memories of those momentary flights; the dip and soar of ramp-riding. As for the bruised collarbone, wrenched shoulder, torn ankle ligaments....Well, a swim is statistically safer, even with the risk of drowning.

Midsummer carries humidity like a sticky clutch bag. I dive, my line shallow and messy, but as I come up, the weir is behind and the river deep and my legs kick out of sight beneath me. Oh, hello unease. Hi, ancient fear. What's it to be today? Dread of my toes brushing something scaly? A Bond movie of piranhas? A rogue, escaped alligator? I try to laugh at myself and squeeze my eyes closed. The water is cool balm. This is going to be a proper, long swim, upstream, all the way out of Ludlow. In the park, children run to the safety rail to stare at the funny man splashing rhythmically past, before parents pull them away with a tut that implies, 'I hope you don't grow up like that.' I don't care. Their imagined disapproval washes right past. The river is the thing, enveloping me, the slow current not even impeding my progress as I follow the alders and willows dripping their leaves onto the surface.

I have swum in the Teme many times, but never this far. As I leave behind the stretches I know, I enter the realms of possibility. Corners, where the river meanders and loops, become exciting zones of transition. What lies beyond? It's the same urge that drives on the walker, the climber, the explorer, the one who seeks answers. And at this moment, anything could lie just beyond my sightline. Anything. Good or bad. Out here I am close to the far country. The fields are full of corn and yellow rape flower, all laid like haphazard pieces of felt over the contours of the hills.

I have an empathic feeling for otters, who are sinuous, who use water as their main travel element, whose skin is the dictionary definition of sleek. I think of the poet Gerard Manley Hopkins and his description of 'liquid-limber youth'. He also talks of the world and how, 'It will flame out, like shining from shook foil.' The pace and pulse of each swum stroke naturally recalls lines of poetry. When I drift near a bank and squish through sinking mud into a field with only cows for company, I glimpse what the poet felt. For my body, just out of the cold water, is garmented with glow and I wander in the green fields. A stand of willows bend against the water, branches hooked against the surface like fishing lines. Shropshire is filled with writers' echoes. We have our own Thomas Hardy, not celebrated enough for my liking, despite the Hollywood rendition of her novel *Gone to Earth*. The novelist and poet Mary Webb still speaks to me, her long-ago verse fresh and verdant:

> Where on the wrinkled stream the willows lean
>
> And fling a very ecstasy of green.

I'm determined to make the least effort in swimming back downriver. It's not hard as the current mostly carries me, the same as it carries twig and leaf and weight of water squeezed from aquifers and rain-soaked hills. Downriver, upriver.

In Shingle Street, Suffolk, my brother Marc and I once scrunched up the pebble beach, tracing the route up the River Ore. We began at the river mouth where it ran fast and tight, sandwiched between spit and land, then followed the flow, backwards. As I drift and swim, Marc is still alive, and we are young men again. We dive into the water, daring to go deeper where the current is a hungry, propelling thrust. There is danger and delight in watching the little gas-lit bungalow we're staying in recede too quickly behind us. The river folds us in its fist, tumbling, turning; we scream with feral joy, not knowing if we'll be spat out to sea; we thrash arms and legs to reach the shore and towels and the hurling of ourselves down to lie still.

We were young, unwise. It was perfect. It's this moment I want for remembering, but he is swept away by the twenty years since I was last with him, when he was gaunt, dying of AIDS, so thirsty, but not able to swallow; his only relief a cotton bud soaked with water and held to his lips. The savage irony of it: of us two water boys, of Marc who loved life.

I love the river and the river loves me. I loved my brother, my only sibling. Yes, there were also resentments and grim times, but they are long gone. I miss him, his playfulness and daring. So I carry him with me back downstream. For if I am the one who has to live on, then he is under me, my water wings, my buoyancy, his words seeping into mine. When I started out as a writer, much of what I wrote was funny, plenty of playful performance poetry, and wordplay for school audiences. Marc, the *proper* poet in my eyes, asked when I would start getting serious. He died. I did, and yet much more than that. As my fingers glide over the keyboard now, like a squash player practising moves in an empty court, perhaps he is ghosting me in the best possible sense. There. He's standing right behind me, resting his hands on mine as I type.

My typing has brought me back to the weir. The teenagers who are making merry have not stolen my clothes, my keys or my cash. Instead, as I rub the circulation back into my feet, they quiz me about who I am and what I'm doing and seem genuinely interested. Stereotypes well and truly dissolved.

Past the old workings of the mill, I find an outdoor table at the Green Café. If there is a God then I'm convinced that he or she did not rest on the seventh day, but came to eat here. Becky, who runs front of house, is warmth embodied and the food is great. I think we're still shocked by good food. But why? Have our palates been restructured to expect that British food is like the mush they serve up on Vexed-Factor-Dine-With-Kitchen-Nightmare? Homemade sourdough bread with a crunchy crust, baked this morning. Call the taste police! It's too damn real. Last time I was here, a couple of blokes came in wanting fish and chips and walked out again when they realised they might have to sit down and be served very reasonably priced, real food. Here, there is lightly grilled salmon with green salad, capers, green lentils followed by boca negra and crème fraîche – the boca negra a melting chocolatey thing that wouldn't know trans-fatty palm oil from recently deceased rainforests if it came up and gave it free liposuction. You can tell the commitment of the staff by the liveliness of the open kitchen and by Clive, who seems to be forever bending over the stainless steel serving point and sprinkling something tasty as he plates up. And the proof is in the café's always being packed and tables needing to be booked in advance. (Being the foodie I am, I've booked.)

As I sit, enjoying sun and food, I realise my relationship with rivers has been repaired. At the first hospital I stayed in last year when I was ill, a river ran not far from the boundaries of the grounds. I was supposed to be 'on observation' for my first few days there, but managed to slip away for a post-therapy afternoon walk along its suburban banks. I think I was hoping that it might help to silence some of the jangling. This was a green strip surrounded by development, yet screened by greenery and trees. I rang my wife as I walked fast, and there was even a moment when I felt vaguely normal: nature bringing brief calm. It didn't last. Later, in the compression of all things clattering and crazy, when my mind was flooded with sick sediment, I hatched a plan for a different kind of submersion. Surely, I mused, if I crept out under the stillness of night and willingly slipped down the bank... if I then went into the water, bent my knees, let the current take me, it would. It would take me far, to the river widening, speeding up, away from the city, through night-valleys and moon-fields, leaving family, love, life behind, until the sea, the great swallower, the mouth of all misery, finally closed over me.

Such a dark dream, except for the fact that the 'river' was only a foot deep. I wanted then, what I achieve now: relief through water. The taking away of aches and pains, mental and physical. Peace. I am so glad I persevered with not-suicide long enough to rediscover that life is, with all its ups and downs, pretty much worth fighting for. Whatever the winter, July always comes again and there shall be, I pray, more good days like this.

River Lugg, Eyton

WE START WITH A MORNING scrubbed clean of cloud, the recent days of grey reduced to small arrows. I wake from a night's sleep that was remarkably free from echoes of my former depression. No three a.m. whisper reminding me that I will grow old and *die*. A very good night. It's Saturday too, even better. Lazy breakfast, coffee and papers. And while we're in the process of stacking up reasons to be cheerful, I find a recipe in the *Guardian* magazine that not only looks good but tallies with what we have sitting in the kitchen. Our neighbour, Kerm – whose garden resembles Mr McGregor's in the Peter Rabbit illustrations – has dropped off a box of beetroot, dug up only yesterday. After scouring, dousing in olive oil, adding smoked salt, garlic and herbs from the garden, I place the beets in the oven. An hour and a half later, with breakfast over, stale bread fried into croutons, and a fresh vinaigrette made with the addition of cumin, the recipe requires only the addition of towels and trunks.

There's no need today for Welsh tarns, or high Scottish waterfalls, not when the borderland is snaked and laddered with clean rivers begging to be leapt into. We all need life maps, though, and mine this weekend is provided by my increasingly thumbed copy of *Wild Swimming*. This time, I hope to find the right spot. It has directions and enticing photos, along with a short description of the swimming in each area. What more do we need? Even Polly, to whom cold water is an enemy to be encountered only in summer, has folded up her swimsuit ready for the battle.

We hit the heat when we step outside, a heavy mattress of it, promising more intensity as the sun bounces higher. We pass Leintwardine, Wigmore, Aymestrey and the picture-book village of Kingsland where the bricks are red and the houses clustered like bees round the old village green. We turn left, seeking smaller lanes, following the course of the River Lugg. Is this it? Is it the right place? There are three cars parked on a verge by a footpath sign.

It has to be it, else why the cars? Anticipation grows as we walk along fields of potatoes. The heat plays tricks, briefly replacing England with the South of France. There's a bank ahead, obviously a flood barrier. Beyond, must be the river. And there's plenty of it. Enough to avoid the group that have set up by the bridge and find our own spot. It is like the process of divining. You walk the length of the river, checking for signs in the surroundings, until a slow curve, over which a poplar rears, speaks to you and says, 'Right here. Here now. Only here.' I take heed of it and blankets and towels are spread out while the water is inspected.

The Lugg has its own reaction to July and lack of rain. It has slowed to slothfulness; tall fronds of algae under the surface wave back and forth in torpid motion. Upriver, sand martins swoop over the water as they dip in staccato swoops to drink and snatch insects on the wing. My old Merrell sandals are falling to bits, but perfect for negotiating the squidgy river bank mud before I can launch and float out into the slow current. The water contains no electric shock today, just a mint coolness. The current is more of a shuffle, so swimming upstream is easy, following the carved-out meander, and keeping my mouth closed to avoid the whirlwind of bugs. Soon, I am out of sight of my wife and son, who wallow and float, close to the bank. It's just me and the Lugg and the noon-fire sun. There's no nip of chill at the extremities urging me to get out. Only the feeling that I could keep going, swim all the way to the shallows of this river, then traipse to the source of the stream.

River Lugg, Eyton

I'm not one to sit on a beach or by a pool for hours on end. I have restless feet, and a fidgety curiosity that has sometimes been the bane of my life. As my family loll in a post-lunch drowsiness, through the heat haze, I spy someone in the far reaches of the field, towel slung over shoulder like a semaphore. I'm intrigued: another swimmer. As the figure makes its way, I walk to intercept. When I was a kid, I hated the way my Czech refugee mum would accost perfect strangers on Hampstead Heath, and within minutes be sharing intimacies of life while I stood there, shamefaced at the idea of *talking* to people in London, *who you did not know.* However, that early role-modelling rubbed off on me and today I'm grateful for the graceful ease with which I have thus made friends over the years. And of course, I in turn embarrass the hell out of our son on a regular basis by daring to talk to strangers. The stranger and I meet in the middle of the field. We immediately chat about great places where good water is to be had and discover that we've both found this one today via the *Wild Swimming* book. She's called Beth, and she has a strong conviction that journeys cross-country must be broken by proper outdoor swims.

She's en route from Bath, away from a friend who chickened out from accompanying her today, and then she'll drive back to Leeds where the anti-river boyfriend waits. She rolls her eyes as she describes a man in love with his armchair, his beer, his TV. Sedentary is the word she tries for size, and I wonder but don't dare say that as an attraction of opposites it sounds, well, unlikely.

Before she takes her leave, Beth suggests the downstream spot she's just found. She describes its feeling of enclosed secrecy. As she dwindles into the green flatness covered in acres of potato plants, I retrace her previous steps towards a stunted hawthorn that marks a bend in the Lugg. In the muddy shallows, where

Demoiselle damselfly

the river is warmed by the sun, a huge shoal of minnows twiddle their tails and, like a flock of starlings, move as one. When I step down, they break and vanish in a breath. I half-float, half-swim downstream until I round a corner, far from family and footpaths, and see that Beth was right. The trees have turned the Lugg into a green hollow-way, a drover's road for the herding of currents. I pause to tread water, am buoyed up in a cavernous glade. A raven flies off in annoyance at the intrusion, his huge wingspan marking him out as 'not crow'. His croak is usually that of too much whisky and cigarettes, but today he is silent. I can't help wondering why, unless he too is caught up in reverence. The damselflies hover and dance. They are such a blue against green, as if their tiny bodies of thorax, abdomen and compound eye, have been beaten out and enamelled by the finest Russian jeweller. I'm truly aloft, a strange sensation of soaring in water, rather than being weighted, and my last thought before I turn back to swim upstream, is a riposte to the three a.m. whisper: death is not to be feared, for all that has been laid to rest is here now, in the peace that passes all misunderstanding.

august

Pantglas

Pantglas, Kerry Ridgeway

I SWAM UP FROM THE DEPTHS LAST NIGHT, having tasted the full moon, distilled its silver. In my dream I was no longer who I am and bark-like age was stripped away. I was a me-in-training for the big day. What on earth? Where dreams are not bound by needing to make sense, I was a mercurial creature, blending free-running and ballet, to whom walls and ceilings were simple surfaces to interact with....

Call this night swimming if you will, the full moon always has an effect on my sleep. It's something our children seem to have inherited too. So the three of us will toss and turn with moon-bit sensitivity, finding that sleep is a wily carp that flicks away just as the hook is about to catch. Then, when I do surface, after finally succumbing, I feel drugged, swaying on the border between day and night. Yeats was fond of these times, believed that if he had his notebook at such transformative moments, he might catch the muse and hold her up, gasping gills shocked at the sudden air.

Now, I've reached the other end of the day: tasks done, meal cooked. The sun is stretching out, easing down, on the last stretch before West. There's something like a doorbell in my mind, and I know where the sound is coming from. It's up on the Kerry Ridgeway and it's very insistent: a pool I haven't been to in ages. I convince Roz to leave her copy of *Hard Times* on her bed, pick up her Canon 5d and head for the hills with me.

The rain gave up an hour ago, after a downpour that beat on our roof as if primeval. It's left a sharpness to the land and a definition in the bulbous slow-moving clouds. All is tinged with the promise of violet late-light. We rise above Bishops Castle, following the old droving route, the Kerry Ridgeway. The house on the side of the lane called Dog and Duck was the original Dog and Duck pub. Back in my TV presenter days, when I was researching the piece about droving, this was one of the old geese- and cattle-trod paths I found out about. It's the pace of the drovers that fascinated me – two miles an hour, six weeks to the rich green grass of Northamptonshire ready for fattening and London. This was *work*, sleeping in a chilly barn if you were lucky, outdoors if not. But oh for the dawdling, the pause to look and see what's around.

These days, we all tend to zip and zoom, windows closed and air-con on. Countryside is something to get through, a space between home and work or school and supermarket. Thus, my job, at this twilight hour, is to fight the urge to get on to the next thing, and the thing in front of that, or to switch on the box of saturated dreams and to turn off the longing of my soul.

We leave the road and crawl up a track, find a verge and lock the car. My tired daughter suddenly understands why we are here. Ten feet in front of us, tarmac ends and the Kerry Ridgeway proper starts. And *ridge-way* is the right description as the land to our right falls away into a haze that only this hour brings. Below lie Churchstoke, the Knuckle, Montgomery Hill. Further still, where outlines are rendered only as the slightest suggestion, the great Welsh Breiddons loom as a dark-shadowed mass.

We follow the rutted track, careless of where our feet land, as the view is so compelling. Around the corner, our goal shines. This is the coin of the realm, the high-water mark dug into the furrows. Perhaps it began with a spring, and surely a farmer in need of water for livestock gave it a helping hand, banking it up with local clay. Yet, this pool sits very comfortably on the lip of a view that Housman would be proud of.

I was right about the timing. Not only is the last of the light gathering itself in soft banks of colour, but everything the sky has to offer is laid out on the pool's rippled surface. Roz has her camera out and she crouches to frame the view, pressing the shutter. An old sheep-dipping gate rusts awkwardly at the edge of the water. It's the perfect position for it to stand, the lines of metal leading out towards the surface. It would make a great photo – and before I know it, I've unravelled my tripod.

'Come on, Dad! The light's going!' Roz is right, as she often is – a bad habit she's picked up from her mother. And I am becoming such a camera-addict that I could quite easily stay working out my captures and keepers until dark steals perspective and I've missed the purpose of our visit.

Trunks on, I walk, or rather scamper, through the cold air towards the far side of the pond. Perhaps pond is the wrong title. It is a lake with self-worth issues, maybe not as massive as its brothers, but perfectly formed nonetheless. Here is a hollow miracle of destruction. In 1941 as German bombers made their way back from the Liverpool raids, they needed to jettison bombs and lose weight quickly. There are craters like this all over the Borderlands, some filled in, some re-wilded with the addition of rain and years to become thriving havens for life rather than death.

Roz won't allow me to leave my towel by the edge as it will spoil her shot. Dammit, I'll be cold when I get out. Still, forget 'out', I need to get in. I wade into the reflected half-light. It is as if the remains of this day have been squeezed to a concentration and poured onto the surface. The mud, no doubt consisting of generations of dead weeds, leaves and various aquatic life, is soft as my feet sink in. Some lakes give off methane at this point, releasing old decomposition. But this little pool has a clean ring to it as I push in, thigh high, then breast-stroke forward.

I've had a few good river swims recently and despite the August heat and general global warming, Shropshire rivers still chill to the bone whatever the time of year. However, this eye of water, staring up at the high-ridged heaven and crowning the border between England and Wales, has soaked up summer. Yes, there's a nip and a delicious shock of weightlessness when I realise the middle has no bottom I can touch. And my skin does tingle with it all as I reach the other side, turning my head to look distance-wards at the command of my daughter. There's also instant understanding. How could I possibly have stayed at home watching the box? So many do; wouldn't be seen out walking or dipping if you paid them with all the light of the world – a currency seeming to bear little truck in these twittering days. But none of it matters. I am suspended above Shropshire, able to see to the horizon as I swim, then dawdle at the very centre of things until the cooling evening impels me to shore.

Once dressed, skin quivering, my heart beating still in the submerged landscape, there is the feeling that all has been captured, all kept. As we drive down out of the hills and into night, we both agree that sometimes it's good to make the effort.

Men's Pond, Hampstead

Men's Pond, Hampstead

I HAVE A STRANGE RELATIONSHIP with London's waters. For me as a child of the Seventies who grew up in the capital, Hampstead Heath was all about the Easter fair: noise, bright lights, the pink spin of the candyfloss machine, fear of the roaming gangs of boys in denim flares and bomber jackets, jealousy of my older brother's girlfriends. In those days, the funfair rides had no acquaintance with health and safety. In one, you would spread yourself around the inside of a huge barrel, which began to spin so fast that eventually you were pinned to the wooden sides. Then the floor would vanish and you prayed to the centrifugal gods you wouldn't drop. Delightful fear was the lake we dipped into as, for those long moments, we defied gravity.

Later, there was skateboarding, punk and dope. Evenings were spread out on the grass, all of London glittering in the distance in a landscape of angular ice. Jokes flowed, ease was toked in shared joints, held in the lungs until nearly bursting, then released into the London air. And finally, when the darkness only left the glowing tips of our cigarettes rising and falling like fireflies, we made our escape, shushing down Haverstock Hill, a purr of polyurethane as we hawks dived in an urban stoop and sought out the soft feather down of stoned sleep.

What did I know then of London's rivers, packed up like anachronistic baggage? All that was left were signifiers – names such as Fleet Street and Sea-cole Lane, lonely typographies that contained meanings no one was still interested in. I had to become a long-term exile before I could look on the place of my childhood and discover it anew. Based in far-off Shropshire, my writing life slowly took to the air, circled round and looked back to find a layered London, all its garish clothes squeezed in tight. But at the bottom of the case, faded, somewhat grey, were clues to less electric times.

A study from the 1980s revealed that in Fleet Road, near the bottom of the Heath, the incidence of bronchitis was higher than in surrounding streets. Basements had problems with damp. That's London all over. If there's space for development and profit, then screw the aesthetics. As for topographical features such as springs, wells and rivers, well when you are done with pissing, shitting, chucking in dead dogs, using the water to wash tripe, to tip out chemicals for leather tanning – in fact, when the River Fleet is no more than a glorified soil pipe – then rein in the banks, canalise it, build over it, bury every trace.

What's left? A few phrases. Keats wrote, 'And then there crept a little noiseless noise among the leaves.' When I was working as a TV presenter filming an elegiac programme on the long-gone rivers of London, we found one of those springs, near to Keats's house, and the poet's voice haunts me still. I love the irony that Fleet Street, once home to the nation's press and the purveyor of journalistic filth, merely echoed the filled-in, sluggish glacier of excrement that the Fleet finally became.

Yet, underneath the dirt, there flow cleaner waters. After World War Two, foundations were being dug for a new house on a bombsite in Kentish Town. From the deep clays an anchor was unearthed. The mind does a double-take, especially if you have ever walked round Kentish Town. The River Fleet, which rose in Hampstead, was sixty-five feet wide at flood in Kentish Town. It was navigable that far up. Imagine it. Boats in the suburbs. In fact, forget suburbs, as Kentish Town was countryside then, far from the Great Wen (London's derogatory nickname coined by

Cobbett in the 1820s. Interestingly, William Cobbett was one of our first naturalists, whose *Rural Rides* became a Victorian bestseller). Further downstream, the Fleet was crossed by seven bridges – an ancient map of London shows the mouth of the Fleet as it empties into the Thames under what is now Blackfriars Bridge. The map shows its proper place in the city as a veritable Venice in miniature. Now, all that flows is the flood of cars on a landlocked sea of tarmac.

But still, the rivers will not go quietly. Go to Ray Street in Clerkenwell and find the grating right in front of the Coach and Horses pub. Listen carefully and you'll hear the flow of the Fleet, now not much more than a well-trained storm sewer lying under the layers of built-up London. Still, the water sings.

These underground rivers also flow through my own personal history. Back in 1951, my grandfather Eduard Fusek, former member of the Czech parliament, owner of a department store in the Wenceslas Square in the heart of Prague, came to Britain with his family. They had all become Czech refugees in 1948 after the Communists stole everything yet failed to catch and execute him. All he had were his hands and his willingness to work hard. In London, he rented a house in West End Lane, just off the Finchley Road. He, who had lost fortune, country, home, language, friends and respect, then discovered that his beloved eldest daughter was dying of leukaemia at the age of eighteen. To survive war and all that loss, to then have this further cruelty. I cannot imagine it.

So, there he was, in a rickety house in the then suburbs, trying to repair frames and broken windows, when wood and glass were still rationed rarities. Anything to make the rooms fit to rent, to make an income, to keep his wife and his second daughter warm and fed. As for that damned basement, why was it always so damp and why did he have to apply to the government for special concrete to cap this instigator of coughs and worse? He was battling nature in striated London. Little did he know that right under the house, another tributary of the Thames flowed. The Westbourne, the little river that also wound across town, which Westbourne Grove is named after, and which filled the Serpentine in Hyde Park before vanishing into the Thames.

When I cross-referenced the map of the lost rivers of London with an A–Z and saw how one of these rivers flowed directly into and under my family's life, I felt a strange shiver – as if I could actually catch history in the palm of my hand and hold it up like storm-tossed amber to the light.

Here today, the light flares and refracts off the Men's Pond in Highgate. I thank the spirits of woods and water that Hampstead was saved from Victorian developers keen to carve it up into villas for the wealthy. And I thank the spirits again. For those very same springs that trickled and threaded across the city of old also made the liquid foundation of the lakes that spread like reflecting lily pads across the Heath. There have been efforts to close the swimming ponds over the years. The good burghers of Health and Safety must have their joy served rare, and eaten with sensible but dull cutlery – for all that glitters is surely dangerous. However, the ponds are still here, havens of wildlife and wild swimming.

I am sweaty from packing books into boxes in my mother's flat, ready for a house move. Books collected into one home over forty-five years fill an awful lot of boxes. The day holds that special humidity London excels at and my body is itchy with dust, formica and old underlay.

The first time I came to the Men's Pond, I was a little confused. The changing area is a large, rough concrete courtyard with a corrugated overhang like a secular cloister. Unlike the mixed pond, there is no grassy area next to the lake to lounge. All that's on offer is this, and the lake itself, with a concrete pontoon and diving board. But oh what a lake! I pause on the pontoon lip to take in the far, tree-filled banks. This is a swimming pool magnified, almost European in its aspiration. Once you jump and adjust to the jolting chill, a leisurely water ramble around the roped-buoy edge is both possible and compulsory. I have swum this pool in March, and managed only fifteen yards out or so before my body began to scream that hypothermia and death really were realistic outcomes. Perhaps I'm just a lightweight, but I am glad this is August, and the chalkboard outside the lifeguard's office says that the water is 68 degrees warm.

This is the opposite of a dip. It's a complete luxurious bathe, this slow breast stroke as I take in the mallards balanced comfortably on a lifebelt ring. They're not bothered by my presence. Why would they be? London can rush all it likes, for here I am cresting the borderland between the city that was, and the home to millions that it now is. Far beneath me, like an underlay, the spring that rises creates a clean freshness. My hands arrow through the surface tension, my skin registering strange patches of water warmed by the sun. I hear the shrill call of a moorhen and right in front of me, indifferent to this huge heron of a man clumsily navigating his way, a crested grebe glides past, wearing its summer ruff of gold. According to the lifeguard blackboard, the grebes are now proud parents! The exclamation mark at the end of the chalky sentence is justified. Here, in the heart of London, life and lives that take no heed of ours just carry on, much the same as all those centuries ago when rivers and people co-existed.

I climb out, towel off, and use the courtyard as the perfect suntrap to warm up. Being in London inevitably reminds me of the tributaries of my own past, when the lure of presenting in front of a TV camera seemed to promise me a life to match the city's glitter. Somehow, like my mother who was an actress in the 1950s, the camera liked my face and viewers also liked what I had to say about history and countryside. One of my fellow presenters was a just-starting-out Julia Bradbury. I wonder at the different lives we subsequently carved out. Ultimately, I found the four-minute-blink-and-you-miss-it sequences too much of a light snack. And it's pretty obvious how much I love a hearty meal! The time I recall today is when I was filming a feature on the lost River Fleet for Carlton Country. I had just shot a segment about Sea-cole Lane, now reduced to a sign next to a modern monstrosity off the main Blackfriars Road. There, sea-coal was once landed. After the Fire of London, the taxes from that coal paid for the building of St Paul's. Truly, such facts are the diamonds that coal sometimes becomes.

During a coffee break from filming, I spotted scaffolding and hoardings right on the route of the Fleet. A camera crew is a remarkable opener of doors and my career has sometimes rested on cheekiness cut with charm. I spoke to the onsite manager and, unbelievably, he allowed us down into the bowels of that building without money changing hands. Down ladders, hard hats on, delving deeper we arrived beneath the basement. This was where excavations had stopped as they had hit a brick wall. Or rather a curved brick obstruction. 'Fleet Ditch,' muttered the foreman. The camera was on, the soundman trying to stop his boom bouncing off the low ceiling as I spoke unscripted and from the heart.

Those words of mine have gone, though I have an ancient

It's hard enough that so much of the Borderlands lies in the hands of the obscenely wealthy; their factory-forest-floor-reared thousands of pheasants, their gamekeepers (who are thankfully not all tarred with the same brush – I've met some great ones) who like nothing better than putting down a nice bit of carbofuran, strychnine or alpha chloralose to give those pesky buzzards, kites and goshawks a meal they will never remember; their big piss-off estates, whose gods are those of the 'Keep Out' variety and who use tripled sections of barbed wire as a form of immigration control so that commoners might not contaminate their acres.

It's hard enough that they have the gall to claim that all this, the air above, the land below, is theirs. But, like feudal lords, they think it is also their right to take a pen and scribble through the dotted green line that was once taken by country kids to school, by labourers too poor for a horse and walking to work, by chapel-goers pouring out from the hills. These lines evolved into the paths that signify our country. We have inherited the majority of those historic paths and enshrined them into the landscape, allowing us to wander them at will. They are the perambulator's Magna Carta, and must be protected, unless we wish to become like the US. Once, while I was staying in Connecticut to work as a storyteller, my hotel room backed onto a small mall, but there was no means to access what was fifty yards away without a car. Going for a walk proved impossible. Though the road and town were surrounded by woods, I couldn't find a single right of way. When I asked about local walks around the environment, people stared at me as though I was crazy. Eventually, I drove a good ten miles to a National Park, the only officially designated walking space.

Today, right in front of me, that legal line has been criss-crossed out. It is subsumed by ferns and barricaded by the holly

Southern Hawker dragonfly

lords of litigation. And I am fuming. I, who in recent years dare less and less to cross an unmarked field. Old walking rights have been replaced with a thicket. I can't go off-piste, must console myself with the rise and fall of pairs of Wood White butterflies, one of our rarest species, with less than one hundred remaining colonies. Well, they might just do OK here, as they are not predators of pheasants, or their eggs.

Instead, I find an alternative route, back through fields, heading down towards the River Clun. On the way, there's time to marvel at and photograph a dragonfly, almost as big as my fist. It's a Southern Hawker and puts me in mind of American drones, which appear to have stolen many of their ideas from a species unlikely to sue. All dragonflies are fairly difficult to capture on camera, but this one does me the honour of landing and staying still momentarily. Easy. A couple of weeks ago, after a swim at Beambridge, a rust-orange Common Darter seemed to take pleasure in teasing me as I pursued it with camera in hand. I worked out that it was making almost the same circuit over and over again and focused manually on a tree it would fly past. I set the fastest shutter speed I could and took endless near-miss shots. Until the final one, framed centrally, transparent gauzy wings frozen and setting-sun painted body pointed at the air like a beckoning finger. Gotcha.

Footpath markings have been eradicated on this route too, but rivers make their own markings, carving valleys and allowing gravity to lead me to their song. I am hot and clammy with walking and though the sun is muffled behind the clouds, the Borderlands simmer with residual heat. Eventually, I draw near but find that the Clun itself is hidden behind layers of new fencing topped with sharp, shiny barbed wire. The fury rises in me all over again until I am just about ready to take a box and stand on Hyde Park's Speakers' Corner to have my say.

However, I re-read the scene in front me and notice the lines and layers of upright, hollow green plastic tubes that denote young willows and alders. I'm the one in the wrong here. The fencing has been constructed to keep out not oiks, but sheep, who love to strip and nibble bark and juicy sap. In twenty years, it will be quite a sight. So, I doff my imaginary cap at this landowner and find another approach to the river.

Plunge time. It may be technically a river, but this stretch is really a deep stream that's suffering from August sluggishness. At the same moment as my foot splashes down, the big mother of all those dancing, shallows-dawdling minnows flashes out of her under-the-footbridge hidey-hole. I get one glimpse, feel the size of that glistening trouty treasure brushing past my ankle, and then she's gone. Patient all these years under the bank, expert avoider of all things bright and hooked, of course she's annoyed at my presence: a big lanky dipper who comes to let all resentment wash away. But there is room for both of us on this muggy day, and it's a pause that refreshes my sense of perspective and sluices my preoccupations.

Later, I learn from Mike Kelly, River Valleys Officer for the Shropshire Hills Area of Outstanding Natural Beauty or AONB (now there's an organisation title that I agree with. It *is* outstandingly, naturally beautiful!) that this stretch of the river once contained and hopes to nourish again a different kind of treasure. What once lay embedded on the river floor in great number, lived for a hundred years, and caused the town of Leintwardine to rise up around the confluence of two rivers, was nothing more than the humble mussel. A special mollusc, it was also one of the reasons why the Romans came – not just for our gold, but our pearls too, forged from a tiny nick of grit in one of a thousand pearl mussels. The great Caesar had a breastplate made of Scottish pearls; armour that was a statement, blaring out the reach of his empire, right to the edge of Europe.

It's not just the threat of poaching for mussels that makes various stretches of the River Clun into Sites of Special Scientific Interest, SSSIs, it's also some modern farming practices. When yields have to be increased and the economy goes to pot, is anyone really going to be thinking hard about a few bivalvular river dwellers? It's an uphill struggle for an organisation's river officer to convince everyone of the merits of changing certain methods. Phosphate, field run-off, the whole dirty mess of it has led to a huge rise in sediment. Waters that ran clear when I started swimming in the Clun so many years ago, now run brown, the pebbles underfoot furred and stained. And yet, the mussels cling on, with the help of people such as Mike and the members of the Shropshire Hills AONB, who are doing their best to save and protect this rare species. What a heritage. Who cannot admire a creature whose larvae dig eight inches into the gravel bed and then spend ten years working their way back up? Some of the mussels then attach to the gills of trout and salmon, growing fatter on the oxygen and nutrient-rich water that passes through. So that's why clean water is required, or else these crustaceans, resembling pairs of hands cupping living history, will be gone, leaving just notes, pictures and dusty old museum jewels, now only good for gawking at.

The tree-planting and barbed wire lining the river takes on an additional significance for me. The trees provide a buffer zone, a line of protection from run-off and chemicals, and animals, a prophylactic for the river. In this instance, fencing is a good thing – a great thing – as it gives our little freshwater pearl mussels a better chance. So, today the river flows a bit more cleanly and I have hope for its inhabitants, including myself.

Afon Artro

september

River Lugg, Aymestrey

River Lugg, Aymestrey

IN THE SPACE OF A FEW DAYS, the air has transformed, carrying an edge with it that hints at the months to come. Last night, after a rather hot and sticky game of squash, and once the rain had clarified the sky and filled the landscape with sharpness again, I stripped off in our tiny backyard ready for an outside shower. Often, when I mention the taking of cold showers – outdoors – to others, the looks I'm met with are puzzled. It is of course the opposite of soothing, warm, power-showered comfort. There is bemused agreement that I must be deluded, despite all the science that tells us that cold water stimulates the immune system and is a most efficacious medicine. But that's not the driving reason why, in summer, I submit myself to daily backyard doses. My little outdoor shower is not, in fact a 'shower' at all, but a tap and hosepipe with sprinkler at the end. For me, it's a portable river fitted with its very own sluice gate for controlling flow. And like my river experiences, after the shock, it offers a cleansing of more than skin and an all-over glow. I recommend it. I might add, for the concerned, that as I towel off, naked, I'm in a secluded spot, overlooked neither by neighbours nor windows. Although I sometimes wonder why my neighbours have let the hedges grow so high....

It works for me, though only in season. Today, when I study the sky and see the angle of the sun growing lower, I know that, even as a cold-waterholic, I will have to put my outdoor showers on hold soon. All is in flux and my drying-off is quick as I am keen to nip back indoors and get some clothes on. I'm even back in socks, for God's sake. What next? Scarves? Hats? I'm tall and thin and my body radiates heat, so yes, winter will dictate my attire as I move towards full muffle mode and let style hang itself as long as I can feel my fingers.

It's not just the year at a turning point. In three weeks' time, eighteen-year-old Roz leaves for university, the girl who slept on my chest the day she was born, with a tea towel for a blanket. Now she is her own five foot eleven skyscraper, always reaching up. The years have not exactly meandered past, but the flow of them has caught me unawares. Here she is, full of books, poetry and wit, and I must take advantage of all I can to eke out these days of her being at home. She is a season, and she will depart and I have no doubt I shall cry and cry.

Today, we are consciously about the business of meandering, all in the cause of Art. H-Art or Herefordshire Art Week is a delightful map of connect-the-dots that sees the Borderlands open up shop, in the form of artists' studios, churches, book binderies and galleries. The cliché of the hills being alive with artists proves to be true.

Roz is on map duty, guiding us through the Clun valley, over the first of the Welsh ranks of sparse hills to Knighton and then beyond to Discoed. There's an old, disused church high on a hill, nestled within what is less a hamlet and more a picturesque flotsam of cottages and barns. Inside, prayers are no longer said, but there are pictures framing the walls that echo the church's stained-glass windows, and there are new original stained-glass panels produced by Tamsin Abbot. These panels illuminate the space as if lit from within. Here is light, framed, and hung on a wire. Tamsin uses glass from the last remaining manufacturer of mouth-blown glass in the UK. The intense blue she works with is created by rolling molten glass at the end of the blowpipe in richly coloured globs called *frit*. Once the glass has achieved the concentration of a Mediterranean sky, it is blown into a long cylindrical bulb, then the ends are cut off and a line cut along the length of the cylinder. The glass is gently heated again so that it can be opened out as a rectangle of flattened glass to make the brittle canvas that the artist can then transform.

The process has similarities to photography. Once the glass is cut with a diamond glass cutter, Tamsin covers the sheet with special glass paint, generally a rich and thick black. When dried, she uses needles, old paintbrushes and sharpened sticks to scrape a negative image, scratching out the spiritual totems of the countryside – Ravens, Owls and the great 'O' of the moon. The prototype is fired at 660 degrees, and the paint, which also contains powdered glass, fuses to the surface. Art is born and today it swings inside the church, firing synapses in my mind and filling my soul with flare. Here is landscape made tiny and, yet, it would be easy to fall into the half-lit hills, to chase that hare through the fields, to listen to the screech of this barn owl. I would love to be the Imelda Marcos of paintings, sculpture and glass and am tempted to buy something. But there are other galleries and installations to seek out in an afternoon where the rain has bowed out gracefully and September light is bringing heat to the tarmac and grass.

On an industrial estate in Presteigne, in a building that can only be described as a unit, we discover an excellent café where the almond and raspberry tart has only just come out of the oven and we sit on ridiculously low sofas reading *Wallpaper* magazine and feeling ever so urban. The hills are filled with the unexpected today and I'm hopeful that this might extend to water. I always sling my trunks and towel into my bag. It's automatic. Besides, I'm keen to stretch the day and the time spent in father–daughter activity for as long as possible. So, after a full afternoon of aesthetic immersion, we're off to pursue something more literal. I've plotted a route across country in search of the higher reaches of one of my favourite rivers.

I feel like Dr Livingstone searching for the source of the Nile, though in a much more modest way. We're looking at the Lugg, barely threading its way through Presteigne, before being joined by Back Brook and Hindwell Brook. These are streams for toe-twiddling, shallow frustrations that laugh in the face of would-be wild swimmers. We turn off the main road, trusting all to the Ordnance Survey map. And immediately, we are in a place of transformation. The road thins, dips beneath high banks as it sinks under the weight of centuries of cattle and cart. These are the old ways that twist and wind around fields, playing follow-my-leader with the valley of the Lugg. It's increasingly noticeable that we've left behind A-roads and probably B-roads too as the way ahead crumbles under the onslaught of wild England. We're not talking the odd pothole here and there, more of an all-out attack, with nature the clear winner. Sure, there is a byway of sorts, but it's crumbly, pitted, the central streak already growing its own miniature nature reserve. There's a sort of time travel at play, whereby it seems entirely reasonable that we might round a corner and find that the tarmac gives up completely, fades into a track or an echo of a path.

We push along a green lane that is more tunnel than right of way, and I stop many times to consult the map. The light is beginning to fall and this adds an air of urgency. *Where* can I find a wallowing place? Maybe I won't – at least, not this high up the river. There really doesn't seem to be anywhere promising. This demands a tactical retreat, back to somewhere familiar; a known quantity: the much-loved stretch of the Lugg, near Aymestrey.

We've never approached this stretch from the head of the valley before, and as it opens out in front of us, we breathe a sigh of relief. We are after the thrill of the unknown and unexplored, yet one doesn't always have to report back from the Mongolian steppes or a yurt in Patagonia. The deepest wilds of Herefordshire also hold their own mythology.

To confirm the rightness of our being here, the late sun is falling directly onto the weir. We hop over the sluice gate, aware of fallen leaves already littering the pebbles, of nettles beginning to curl, of the much-mentioned-because-it's-bloody-everywhere Himalayan balsam beginning to wilt.

Once we've changed into our swimwear, there is only one way to approach it. I'm at the lip of the weir again. The top of the weir was completely dry when we crossed, as the heavy rains have yet to come and refill the river. This means that the water in front of me is shallow, maybe three or four feet, so I will have to jump and make it a careful entry, feet first, then curl my body up to avoid hitting rocky bottom. A sort of clumsy, free-runner's vault. Roz holds my camera, determined to capture the moment, the dare when I'm not forty-eight but eight. I jump. There is a single, weightless split of a second before the Lugg claims me. All is suddenness, and the freshness of early autumn spills over my head. The river knows all. Like the air, she carries what's to come and can't pretend to a warmth that was only just acceptable in July and August. We both dip, daughter and I, diving, ducking, swimming, leaping from the River Lugg, glad of it all. Glad we are here. Glad we can rise and fall, over and over: rise from the river; climb out; stand and fall in again. It's as though we are playing the same reel of film. I have time on a loop that I don't want to break, because in each moment of landing under the water, even as the splash rises, everything slows and is still and unchanging.

In my late teenage years, I had my Hermann Hesse phase. He spoke then to my yearning spirit as his book *Siddhartha* does now: 'They both listened silently to the water, which to them was not just water, but the voice of life, the voice of Being, the voice of perpetual Becoming.'

I grasp the moment, but I can't hold it. The current trundles on when I rise up and hop onto the weir for the last time today. And then I'm glad too that, once Roz has changed, I can turn the camera on and catch her frame by frame, using all that the late light and trees and water have to offer.

We have grabbed this day and stretched it, spun it like glass – condensed all the colour into a great shining.

Pistyll Rhaeadr Waterfall, Wales

I FEEL I AM BEING FUNNELLED, that this month is the pouring out and filtering of scraps from a season that is rapidly vanishing behind us. The day starts well with an early mist unable to win against the rising sun. But, as we head across the border and thread through smaller roads in the hills behind Welshpool, the light becomes migratory, fleeing to warmer climes. I have to check myself at this point; after all, we live in a country whose social conversation would be depleted if there wasn't so *much* weather to discuss, where the default colour for sky is muffled grey. I'm British. I should *know* these things. Weather is as weather does. And now it's doing rain.

Polly drives and we've managed to persuade Roz along for the ride too. We try to pinpoint when we last made this trip and

Pistyll Rhaeadr

recall that it was when our now thirteen-year-old son, Asa, was a baby in a car seat and the elongated eighteen-year-old beauty of a daughter in the back was a child. Instead of wielding a Canon 5d to snap the landscape, she was creating watery fairy dens with miniature copies of My Little Pony.

Beyond Llanrhaeadr-ym-Mochnant, the road becomes a track, skirting the Afon Rhaeadr, in response to the steepness of the valley sides. Perhaps it was this sense of a hidden micro-climate that got the Romans planting grapes here, the Tannat grapes the valley is named after. Now a sheep-spotted wilderness, it's extraordinary to think of this Welsh nook as a major wine-producing region.

One more twisty corner negotiated and above us rise the falls, all 240 feet of them, higher than Niagara with an impressive gravity of shining spray. George Borrow described it better than anyone:

> What shall I liken it to? I scarcely know, unless it is
> to an immense skein of silk agitated and disturbed by
> tempestuous blasts, or to the long tail of a grey courser
> at furious speed. I never saw water falling so gracefully,
> so much like thin, beautiful threads as here.

There is something immensely satisfying about the falls being an end point; the road has no choice but to come to a full stop. The car park and Swiss-style chalet-café sit well, overlooking the lip of the river. The water is already compelling – as I open the car door, I can hear the roar of it, the voice of all that volume, singing as it plummets. Perhaps the air is ionised, but there is freshness to every breath. Swim first, or pictures? It's a hard one. I take all my kit nevertheless. The route to the base of the fall includes a clambering sequence over rocks that are smooth, wet and very keen to mess with ankles. Tripod in one hand, camera in the other, I am a tottering picture-taker, not keen on broken limbs today.

The waterfall rears above us, its high rim almost bleached out by the grey light. Halfway down, there is a hole in the rock, suspended vertically like a giant, lichen-painted Polo, a mouth through which the River Pistyll speaks. The pool at the bottom is suddenly revealed, a lovely, constantly undulating *O*, resting for a moment before the river continues its ride. The weather has done us a favour. For the steep woods on my right are often as packed as any Brighton beach in high summer. Polly reminds us of a long-ago trip when she squeezed and balanced herself into a last inch of space under a tree, heavily pregnant with our son. At the time, she was desperately trying to finish writing the last few scenes (by hand) of one of our early published plays, *Much Ado About Clubbing*, while I entertained small Roz and cooled off in the water.

And today, after all those years, cooling off is what I'm about to do again, in spite of the light spits of rain having just worked up into a steady drizzle. I cover my already set-up camera kit with my waterproof coat. Rain may hold up photography but not swimming, so I change fast and paddle through the shallow depths of the pool, towards the torrent of white water that turns to white noise in my ears. I'm in up to my thighs and surprised that it's not killer cold, am even lulled into thinking that this might be both a dawdle and a doddle. Once the water is above my waist, it's the moment to sink back into the falls, one of the 'Seven Wonders of Wales'. This river is called Afon Disgynfa, Disgynfa meaning: a place where falling or descent takes place.

So this is what I am doing, descending slowly into the bubbled netherworld, the wash of water shaping a band of hard volcanic rock. I fall through Ordovician mudstones, shales and slates of the Caradoc series with bands of acid lava and the delightfully named rock called 'tuff'. This is no silky drop, though. It is jolt and shove and the body-blow of hurled river. It is stone and fire and water and holding my breath as I am suspended in history. Not for long. The pummel and pounding, the magnificent might, the elemental weight pushes me forwards and I leap up, arms raised, the tingling of my skin an alarm bell issuing all sorts of dire health-and-safety warnings. This is no time to just man-up. I have dipped, letting the force of the fall tumble and roil me, and now I want shelter: land and dryness. I enjoy the melodrama, running – or rather, fast-waddling while yelling – from the water. No shame in the brevity of it, only joy that I tasted the plummeting river this morning. It is enough.

Perhaps my immersion has worked a totemic magic; appeased the sky gods a little, as they relent and – in condescending but beneficent manner – temporarily cancel the rain. Whilst submerged, and this happens more and more these days, the framing for the camera shot I want suddenly becomes obvious to me. There is a massive tree trunk lying at the edge of the pool like a fallen, shining giant. With that as my foreground, and the great white spume as backdrop, things are going to work out very nicely.

There is more serendipity too, or perhaps the rumoured fairies in the wood really have sprinkled a bit of quartzite dust over the proceedings. As I fiddle with my kit as only an obsessed man can, another cagouled gentleman of uncertain age begins to take an interest in what I am doing. We get chatting, first about the shot itself. We both wonder aloud where the tree came from. But in 1966, Germany, when my father was still alive, still laughing, still drinking coffee; before that morning when he set off to his office in his orange Porsche and never came home again.

What tools did my father have to help overcome depression? The love of my mother and the best that 1960s pharmacology could muster. Alongside that, there were the interventions of his own father, who helpfully reminded him that it was all his own fault when the company had a seemingly crippling tax bill to pay, and who told him that he was a failure both as a son and as a businessman. My paternal grandfather was not known for his gentleness. His own mental-health issues often saw him take out his shotgun during family arguments and stalk off into the woods, threatening to put an end to himself. He didn't, but my father took that paternal lesson to heart and believed the generational lies passed down. He was unable to change the patterns in his mind.

Despite my own suffering, there were many lifebelts thrown to me along the way. During the process of my recovery last year, I was offered an NHS six-week course in CBT and mindfulness. One of the exercises involved sitting in a room with a bunch of screwballs-like-me and eating strawberries, which we tried hard to 'taste' and 'smell'. Sounds like a waste of taxpayers' money? Absolutely not. One of our number had lost the ability to go out, being so afraid of going mad and harming someone. It was obvious to everyone else that this was never going to happen, but the person in question believed their stream of dark thoughts. It was the reality of those thoughts that the course began to challenge. A severely depressed person becomes so caught up in fear, anxiety, thoughts of death, a sense of doom, in failures real and imaginary, that all present experiences fade. No wonder that, in depression, one of the many symptoms is being unable to taste food. The NHS course made a difference, a huge one. Even now, I can watch one of my favourite forms of thought-torture – 'You're going to die, so what's the point?' – and let it drift away. The Buddhists have it right: be here now. (Though I still love Steve Bhaerman's creation, Swami Beyondananda, who says, 'Be There Then!')

Diving into wild water is the great bringer-back of reality. A perfect present tense, a right-here, right-now moment. The senses are so filled by the trees, the light, the sound of birds, of shivering leaves, the fierce, squeezing clinch of water – there's no space for thought shadows.

Once dry and clothed, a thermos of hot coffee helps warm me up. As I drink my nicely bitter brew, I think back to our find of Kafino 1002 Kaffeefilterpapier. The company, like my father, is long gone, but here we are in the middle of Wales, sipping a surprisingly smooth coffee dripped from filter paper that began its life in the kitchen of Hildesheim where I was born. When my mother lost her beloved, and left Germany to begin a new life in London with her two young boys, she brought what she could with her. Strange how a brand name can carry so much resonance.

River Onny West, Nind

I WOKE THIS MORNING to the scent of burning leaves, the pungency of summer making a mist of its own that has wrapped itself round our house, courtesy of Kerm next door who is ever the early riser. His instinct – to gather up the season and give it a fiery send-off – is spot on. For there is mist of a different kind hanging around, a thickness the sun is struggling to punch through; signs of change. Even the swallows are nervous, gathered in great congregations on the phone wires and then, by some invisible signal,

River Onny West

all taking wing at once. Soon they, like the late warm days we are being treated to, will be gone.

There's an urgency that comes with change, and today it's murmuring a name in my ear: 'Snailbeach.' So here I am, map spread on table, finger hovering like a divining rod. My photographer friend Ray has told me that Snailbeach pool has been refreshed, dredged and naturally filled with rainwater once again. But the map has a plethora of blue colouring-in. Which of these blobs is the pool? There's only one way to find out.

The day is mixing it up. Is it still September, or are we already veering into October? Certainly, the air has cooled, driving in from Russia and forcing the wearing of slippers. I make no apologies for my indoor footwear: being six foot eight, my feet are a long way away and my circulation registers the season.

But weather has never been my deterrent. Even better, as I zip along the A488 now towards Minsterley, I spy a sign that reads, 'Snailbeach open day.' This former mining community has a wealth of heritage buildings on a site managed and preserved by Shropshire's outdoor recreation service and the Shropshire Mines Trust. There are restored buildings to explore and today there are mine tours on offer too, courtesy of the Shropshire Caving and Mining Club.

What nobody mentioned, I reflect after an hour and a half spent crawling through tunnels, is that these passageways weren't built for the lanky. But I'm not complaining. Back in the nineteenth century, ore-mining was incredibly hard, the only light provided by candles, the only way to retrieve precious minerals from their seams a pick and the odd explosive or ten. There was constant danger of cave-in, or flooding in the lower levels. Nor could the mine company be relied upon in those pre-safety-conscious days to give a damn. On 6 March 1895, the rope that lowered the workers into the depths of St George's shaft failed. A seven-foot-six-high cage was crushed to eighteen inches. Seven men lost their lives, but, crucially, the inquest determined: 'Accidental death caused by breakage of a defective rope.' There was no compensation. One bizarre detail stands out amidst all that tragedy: one of the mineworker's watches was untouched and still ticking.

We are down in the deeps, breathing a silent, unstirring air. Puddles and mud are slippery underfoot and the rock about us is not smooth, but gouged. Without my helmet, I'd have a bashed head by now. We are now within a high, natural fault that is cavernous in size. Here, the miners scrabbled upwards to follow the sparkling white vitreous veins of barytes. All that's left of their work are a few rotten planks of timber sticking out of the rock like accusing fingers, the remnants of ancient platforms. We are surrounded by the statues of ghosts as we imbibe ancient sorrows.

Of course, there are further levels, but you have to abseil down to reach them. Our guide, Andy, says it might be possible to come back later this year and delve further with my camera. I wonder about layered wild swims, enfolded in the earth, yet still drifting downriver. When we finally stumble into the afternoon light, I blink with the brightness of it. Fair play to those hard-working men who brought out the ore. An additional strange fact I've learned during the tour is that barium ore is used as an additive for paper pulp. I muse that, as an author, my hand has stroked the mineral surface and seen its transformation into the landscape of words.

I am hot, damp and my curiosity is satisfied. Once more, I'm an Alice who, having visited another strange Wonderland, has popped back out of a rabbit hole. Of course, an open day wouldn't be entirely complete without cake, and the locals of Snailbeach all into a soft and tired shade, thankfully still a long way from the harsh dark of winter.

It is no more than a stream, with tight five-foot meanders, wriggling along the shallow valley. Each corner, each curve is the geological product of winter floods about their work, impelling puffed-up currents about their business of imitating JCBs. The force of water and suspended silt has carved out the land, leaving these hollow bowls to brown trout and mad wild swimmers. I decide the sheep will not be offended if the skinny man skinny-dips.

Actual swimming will not be an option here due to the shallowness. I must lie bank and sink of England. Delightful. The cold suffuses me, around me, sluicing past. My outspread fingers are water-weed, rippling. I'm about to jump up and get dressed when I hear a car slowing on the lane. Then a thought floats to me. Where exactly am I? Am I on a landed estate? If it's the one I'm thinking of, then while I'm sure that its owner is the perfect gentleman, it's an estate with an excessive number of 'Private' signs. A woman who has lived most of her life on a cottage adjoining this land told me that the old river pool by the house was much frequented in the days of a previous owner. Generations of local children were taught to swim in it. But now, signs are neatly printed and the delighted squeals of the young have been banished to oral history. So, as I lie low, very low as it happens – hidden below the bank and the trees – that familiar fear rises in me. What if it is the man himself, or his keeper, suspicious of a car parked in the lay-by with no oik around to account for himself?

The car drives off, thankfully also carting away my fears. What's left is only a frisson of naughtiness. Am I really allowed to have this much fun? I dress and feel glad, bow in appreciation to the stream that dreams of being a river. Then I run back through the field, keeping a lookout for joy snatchers, although I am the one snatching summer from the inevitable jaws. Cows low in the distance, their baritone reverberating. The song of the alder leaves in the wind joins with that of the River Onny West, the tiny tributary of a watercourse I have explored over twenty years, but never this high up. Truly, I have come close to the source. All is calm, all is good. And at home there is curry to make and our son to organise for a sleepover. Much battling will no doubt be had with his mates on computer screens, much pizza devoured, much laughter ringing round our house, which was once a chapel and is a place of spirit still.

Holt Fleet Bridge, River Severn

LATE YESTERDAY AFTERNOON, the summer briefly reappeared and I found myself walking in vast woodlands near Crowthorne, Berkshire. I was there for an author event, but was sat twiddling literary thumbs in the hotel when the sun crooked its fingers and invited me out. After a sludgy start, the day was ridiculously hot – as if September was having an identity crisis. As I strode up a wide ride with stands of pine and scrubland dominating the view, I spied a nearby glint. Yes, it was a somewhat public place, but water is water and must be snatched where it can. I came over a small rise, only to find bare and scorched earth, a vast plastic drainage pipe and a pool that had infectious diseases written all over it. I am committed to the concept of *wild* swimming, but this sterile piece of dead water was not it. Instead, I diverted from the path and picked my way up less trampled routes. And there, startled, but not yet bolting, a light brown head and shoulders peered with ridiculously round eyes from the high grasses.

Of course I had my camera with me, but I'd been editing my last shots and the card was still stuck in my laptop. Oh bloody joy. Still, as my daughter says, not everything is a photograph. Meanwhile, I mimicked this wonderful burnt-red doe of a deer, becoming simply another tree on the spot, no movement within me, no threat. The doe's ears could not go any higher. She could see me, knew I was there, wondered what I was. And what I am is still young enough to allow myself wonder at this co-existence; this wild, fence-jumping shyness that still survives despite the cockroach-like encroachment of car and wilderness-leavening architecture. We had a few seconds together, and then she exited stage left.

This morning, the sludge has returned with a grey vengeance, but I can't complain, as I am sharing my pot of Darjeeling with one of my heroes, author Philip Reeve. He is dapperly dressed and somewhat shy, but happy to swap tales of editors and school visits. All I keep thinking is, *this is the man who got my son reading* and whose Mortal Engines books took steam-punk to an entirely new level. Having grown up in London, here I was reading about a London of the future, *on wheels*. In his books, the big cities of the world have evolved to move, like great layered cakes of menacing but beautiful architecture, which trundle round the empty oceans on huge caterpillar tracks, hunting down smaller towns and hamlets to tear apart for fuel and slaves. Reeve calls it Municipal Darwinism, and any man who can create a phrase like that is very much all right by me.

The day is full of words punctuated by refreshments in a café set up in the school and which features unbelievable homemade cakes baked by one of the parents. Chocolate and hazelnut helps

Holt Fleet Bridge

me recover from the adrenaline of performing and gets me ready for the four-hour trek home. I have trunks and towels and as I gain the Midlands and leave the south behind, once again the good weather befriends me and fills my mind with the glittering lure of dipping. There are spots I know where I could stop off, but that's sometimes too easy. I feel a bit like the fisherman who catches the same carp in the same pool over and over again, but who has heard tell of a lake where the carp breed like monsters and the access is both illegal and dangerous. We always want what's round the corner. Out of sight is part of what drives us as human beings. So, let's forget what's safe.

Now motorways have been negotiated, and a bitter flat white brew from one of the biggie, infamous coffee chains drained down my throat purely as an energy additive. (Yes, I admit to the hypocrisy on all counts but where's a writer to find a proper, serious coffee these days at the corporate squeeze-wads that pass as 'service' stations?) However, the coffee keeps me awake and takes me all the way to the bypassing of Worcester and, at last, the Holt Fleet Bridge that crosses the Severn.

I have driven this way many times and always thought it looked interesting, but couldn't see a spot to park my car. Also, when I hear the words River Severn, I generally shudder, remembering an exploration round the back of Welshpool many summers ago when I was desperate for watery relief. Every time I found a path that led to the Severn, what I also found was a banked-up watercourse (to prevent flooding) that looked forever like a great swollen bowl of the brown stuff. Good for kayaking, but perilous for a flailing body. Not inviting all round, and common sense has kept me from it since. However, this area, further downriver by a couple of counties, looks different.

First, I swing into a small supermarket, where enough booze is on low price special offer to encourage its very own alcoholic epidemic. I do wish these high-discount business models would be honest in their advertising: 'Come get liver disease here!' Or, 'Keep drinking: screw up your relationships, your kids, your job. Three for the price of one!' Heaven forbid that the government should actually dare to raise the price per unit of alcohol, as recommended by most health experts. We wouldn't want to lose all the tax revenue, would we, so perhaps the massive cost to the NHS and to destroyed families is a worthy sacrifice to the god of commerce? I'm not actually anti-alcohol, far from it – my friends enjoy a drink, as do my family. The key lies in the word 'enjoy', as opposed to alcohol being a means to an end.

I carry my inner 'Grrrr' with me from the store, along with a carton of juice and a couple of apples, and make my way upriver past the fishermen and the helpful 'No Swimming' (or you die) signs. The proliferation of signs along the length of the waterway, beyond the short stretch of locks that lie like so much wonderfully preserved heritage on my path, strikes me as strange, especially when the Severn is full of pleasure craft. If they are allowed in these waters, then surely my smaller vessel of skin, bone and heart should make no nuisance? But I decide not to rock the literal boat, instead removing myself from the sight of all the potential tutters and finger-waggers. This part of the river has a plethora of small wooden houses and chalets that look like they might have started life as shacks but have been craftily expanded over the years. Like me, the shorts-wearers lounging on house decks are after the same prize – the last gold of summer, the precious warmth in the air, the damselfly iridescent blue of the sky.

It's crazy good weather and already I feel glad to have broken my journey. The motorway and its lifeless air have been borne away and I'm breathing in clean breezes, aware that the locks, the danger signs and the habitations are suddenly behind me. Now it's the time to look for a way down the steep bank and into inviting water. A little further along lies a crescent-moon tiny beach cut into the clay. This will do. Here is a gap among the hawthorn and willow, my entrance to that rich loam of river. I am still standing on the footpath, so change ridiculously quickly and step carefully towards the edge. As the water is mud-brown rather than clear, there is the inevitable moment of hesitation before wading on; the what-ifs of under-surface obstruction or aquatic shopping trolley dragger-downer. I just have to take it slowly and gently, feel my way forward. The water is at that delicious midway seasonal point of being neither warm nor cold. Then I am out, away from the bank, strolling the slow currents with arms and legs, happy as a land boy who has discovered more to life than mere solidity.

A cruiser chugs past, and I wave at the people on it with a stupid grin on my face. It's smiles all round, for who cannot be happy on a day like this? I linger, tread water, watch a coot scoot along under overhanging branches, dawdle as the Severn goes about its business, basking under the month's sunshine, pleased with its own splashy harmonics. All in all, this is my equivalent of resting overnight at a hostelry. I have been plied with good refreshments and a restoring bath and am ready to continue my journey.

october

River Lugg, Bodenham

River Lugg, Bodenham

I T WAS JUNE 2003. I had not seen my old school friend Charlie
for very many years, so there we were, meeting up at the Mixed
Pond on Hampstead Heath – his idea. It took a moment to work
them out, the man who stood before me and the boy within my
memories. His hair had fled to the borders and belly expanded
with the fullness of living. But in those eyes lay the puckish mate I
knew. What were the years since last we met? Evaporations, water
under the bridge of middle age on which we both stood and from
where we took in the view.

Although the sky was overcast, London and Hampstead
Heath contained enough warmth to satisfy my bare skin. For
this water, there had to be no half-measures. As we leaped from
the jetty, there was a squeeze of a moment between anticipation and shock, and I was truly surprised. In all the years I had
spent growing up in London, I had never known of this place, this
spring-fed delight, this River-Fleet-motherlode.

We swam a slow, meandering circle of the lake, marvelling
at our ability to spy moorhens and mallards on the same level as
ourselves. Then we climbed out and dried on the tiny patch of
grass that, come high summer, would be as packed as St Tropez,
and talked of all the time that ebbed behind us.

Charlie really was my first best friend, the jazz-hands man who
tootled out a post-prep tune in the common room of our boarding
school, and who, years later, risked the stage one afternoon with
seasoned musicians at Dingwalls in Camden Town. Despite the
sunshine outside that day, the innards of the club were black and
smoky. Atmosphere and music was all. His hands were shaking
as he climbed the tiny podium, but he did it nevertheless.

He had shared my white-water descent through spliff, bong, chillum, and on over darker acid rapids and into whirlpool swirls of too, too much speed. How many evenings had there been when our giggles had slowly drowned in numb unconsciousness, how many stumbled staggers home to sleep the unknowingness of the dead? Until I was whirled away at sixteen into a psychiatric ward, with those we called schizos, downers and suicidal girls. I had fitted in rather well, being somewhat unwell myself.

When my housemaster came to see me, all I could say was 'I'm so confused'. Because I was underwater, could see the upper world only through a glass reflected darkly, and wondered how the normal people with the A–Z of life managed every day. I look back now and laugh like a loon at the fact that I actually believed every book in the unit's library was written about me. I was adrift and very lost in the murk of my own dark imaginings.

Amazingly, I did not drown. Some small spirit burned deep, some need for air and life; some helping hand buoyed me up. But it took time – six months off school. By then, Charlie had left and moved on. Only now, as we sat by this lake in London, yet in the heart of all things flowing, fresh and green as only June can make them, did I learn that his twenties had also taken him down. Sectioned, mad, lost. We could have been identical twins in the realms of suffering. However, and this is what I loved him for the most, Charlie, like the wily carp who fights the hook, would not give up so easily. Out of that impossible turbulence, he had grabbed and gained a freedom once again, had made a life, had a child, a second wife and a good job, working to support troubled families. I only recently found out how, when he arranged to meet up with me that day at the Mixed Pond, he'd been as excited as a child that we had found each other again.

It seems our friendship had much water in it. Rolling forward through the years, I wrote a poem for his second wedding; he and she came to stay at ours with Charlie's son from his first marriage; he cooked us wonderful spicy noodle dishes doused in chilli oil; we all walked in hills, on beaches, by lakes. But then, after more years, there was a dark December day by which time he'd misplaced his beloved. Things had not worked. She had left and he was broken in a way I'd never seen. We walked at dusk on the beach at Barmouth. Because the sand was damp, Charlie held my clothes when I decided that the sea needed my company. My stay in that frigid smudge was short to the point of screeching. But I did it nevertheless, got my fix of glow-gladness, changed and we walked on. At that point, he told me that his drinking had laid him low, and wondered if I could help.

I never trumpet my recovery from alcoholism and addiction, but nor do I hide in shame from the facts of what I was – and still could be – were I to pick up another drink or drug, even after getting on for thirty years clean and sober. Part of the price, the heavy gift of what nearly broke me but led me to find help to repair, is that I must give it back. I have to fall out of my self, my ego, my own worries, step outside everything and try to give a hand to others who are going through the same struggles I once suffered. I so wanted Charlie to see his way out and to discover that his spirit of humour and joy and stubbornness and great individuality would be made no less by putting all that shit down. Recovery has made me *more* myself, *less* conforming, further able to go in the directions my spirit suggests.

Here's the nub of it. Charlie carried on working, gained his social work degree, added greatly to the lives of un-healed others, the broken children – products of other parents' alcoholism and addiction. Yet he could not heal himself. When the email from his sister came, I could not breathe. It seemed impossible. The details were uncertain, but whatever the circumstance, it was wrong. He had gone. He was my age: forty-eight, an age where newness is still possible and where life can easily begin again. It should not be an age that is the summit, where we miss a step, where ravines await. It is like the car reversing on a motorway – which my grandfather did once in Washington DC when he was well into his eighties, my mother and I trembling like jellyfish in our seats, aware that the natural order of things was in danger of suddenly crashing down. We survived. Charlie didn't.

One week later, we are in the Jewish cemetery at Willesden Green and I am hearing all about the facets of his life from brother, sister, nephew, boss, and me, the weeping poet. Why, when it must make my living wage, do I also have to mark the loss of friends and of family with words? Because it feels mandatory. I have to: it's a duty. The night I heard that Charlie had died I couldn't sleep. I rose too, too early and felt the verses rising like a spring. There was no choice, but to rise also, speak my piece and make my peace.

Here are rivers, in this tiny modest hall, filled with wept salt. Then I am done and stumble back to my seat. When the coffin has been lowered into the pit, and family and congregation members throw their waterfall handfuls of earth, the rabbi takes us back for final prayers. 'He maketh me lie down in green pastures. He leadeth me beside still waters.' And she reminds us that there is a small basin on the way out and that we are welcome, both Jew and Gentile, to wash our hands if we wish. The water is the symbol, and our act a way of marking our transition from departing the place of death to entering that of life once more. Yes, finishes the rabbi, you must grieve, but also you must live.

I am stunned. There is much wisdom here. It's a good place for Charlie to rest, next to his father. There are trees and a glimpse, far away, of distant hills that are Not-London. He'll even have Michael Winner for company.

So, I take the rabbi to heart. As we head home later that weekend, the motorway slows like the chug-a-long and we divert, skirt Ledbury and cross Herefordshire on the A417. This Indian summer keeps returning like a welcome, brief visitor and the late-afternoon haze is filled with blue. There's a spot on the Rver Lugg I have not visited for years, mainly due to forests of ridiculously tall nettles that make access impossible. But the nettles have begun to give up their grip, their sting wilting like their leaves. Fallen, pink petals line the banks as I skirt round the edge of a field of frisky bullocks – who snort and gallop off at my presence. The river turns, and there's an old and crumbling weir. I climb the barbed wire fence, descend through alders and yellowing willows, their little curled slivers of sun floating downriver. All is change, but here is the compression of the months behind us, one last squeeze that is sweet and tangy.

I can tell it is a long-frequented place as the bank is filled with old glass bottles, many Victorian. Uncollected, tarnished chuck of history. Alongside are their more recent, rowdier brothers, decked out in unbiodegradable plastic, presumably thrown by those who have forgotten how to care. My grief is instantly heavier as I wonder what a world it is when those whose souls are sightless can desecrate beauty with such terrible ease. However, not even rubbish can spoil the clean and clear moment when my feet slip and slide across the weir.

I do as the rabbi commands. I turn, fall backwards, am fully taken into the grace of the river and am washed, made by this cold flow into life's current once again. This is the moment, the dare, the risk, the symbol of all that fighting, laughing, loving spirit of my oldest mate. This one is for you, my friend. Bless you, Charlie. Stay safe and, as you used to say with the grin that is yours and yours alone: stay cool.

Oakley Mill Waterfall, the Long Mynd

I HAVE BEEN IRRITABLE FOR DAYS, like an addict in withdrawal. Perhaps it's the knowledge that daughter Roz is soon to leave home for the far shores of university. Whatever the reason, I'm a contrary bugger this morning. Drawers deliberately attack my shins, and family members are berated over the smallest infraction. Roz for forgetting to deal with a few dirty mugs in her room is a good example. As she points out, many teenagers are busy doing far worse. Her supposed sins are meek in comparison and even I can see my snippiness is out of proportion.

Over the last few weeks, each time I drive I feel imprisoned in my car. The sun beyond the window, with its hints of summer-behind-us-now, is taunting me. The recent rains have done my mood no favours, in their rinsing of the farmers' fields, sluicing all those spray-ons into the watercourses and then into the rivers that are usually my habitat. The Clun, the Onny and the Teme, liquid thoroughfares of this borderland, are currently ugly and swollen in spate. Dark, doily swirls pattern and pucker the speckled brown surface, promising currents within currents and treachery Shakespeare would be proud of. You don't mess with water in this mood, whose invisible depths I have mapped with footholds that have been wiped out and where river banks have vanished into thin, misty air.

Oakley Mill Waterfall

When I was younger, I would occasionally swim such raging torrents, out of a bravado of immortality that lingered long into my twenties. Danger tasted like iron on my tongue. 'Swim' was an optimistic word, when currents slammed me downstream in what felt fast as flight. Obviously, I lived to tell the tale, despite my stupidity, but my skin told another story – always instinctive, reacting against all those nitrates mixed up in a soup of mud and bringing out my body in an all-over rash, as if I had bathed in nettles. These days, I try to be more measured, though the urge still floods me. This early October morning, when the clouds are half and half and the sun dips in and out like a swallow, I feel my mood begin to soar.

We head for the high places, Roz and I, once I have apologised for being a ratbag. Our mission is to delve on foot into one of the deep glacial valleys called batches that furrow the side of the Long Mynd. It's named on the map as Small Batch, as are several of the parallel valleys, though 'small' cannot contain these massive ramparts of scree and grass that rear above each side of the brook towards the sky. Here, we are high enough to avoid field run-off. The ridges around have soaked up the rain and squeezed it like a sponge so that the hills are dripping with springs and streams, brooks and burns. It's hill country, quartered by kite and buzzard, not a good or safe place to be lost in fog or snow.

The waterfall has been in my head since I went to bed last night, cradling the thought of it through the landscape of my dreams. Autumn swims carry with them the scent of rule-breaking. Am I allowed to stretch summer out into these shortening days? Here we are in the Borderlands, grass dew dampening our boots, also treading the precarious ledge that lies between seasons. The car is soon lost behind us as we wade through acres of ferns, already dying back to yellow before finally curling into their own brown mortality, brittle as old papyrus. The walls of the valley close in, the path no more than a thin, sheep-trod thread. The stream accompanies us, more spindly with each step, its hum a burbling suburb of sibilance. The stream narrows, then curves, forcing us to scramble over rock and look down over the pool on our right, a round, frothing 'O'.

A certain Thomas Wright of London came here in 1877 and decided that his description of a family outing, with picnic, warranted a book, which now rests submerged deep within the Shrewsbury Archives. What a joy to set my hook, bait it with curiosity and land the rich language and experience of another time:

> Here we enter a lovely valley closely bordered on each
> side by picturesque hills rising into mountains, here
> clothed with rich foliage and there rising in barren
> masses, and down the side of which trickle innumerable
> streams of water filled with trout and other fish.

Well, here I am, edged on one of those very streams, the time
between me and Thomas Wright thin as a sheet of paper. I can
feel my heart speed up. I change, aware of how weak and low the
sun is, barely warming my skin. Clambering down, I plunge first
one foot, then the other onto the submerged, slippery stone of
this rock-carved hot tub, without the heat. The temperature of
the water is like a warning. Do not approach! Danger! How am
I supposed to look relaxed as I fold up and submerge myself?
My daughter is peremptory. Camera focused, she reminds me
that grimacing is not photogenic. So I swallow down my cold
agony, and practise an air of floating insouciance for about three
seconds.

In this short space, I contemplate this happenstance of
curling stream and resistant dolerite rock. The meaning of the
word 'dolerite' needs to be looked up to understand its volcanic
source. Here once was fire, the molten forging of landscape. But
then came the cold craftsman. From millions of years, we move
to thousands; this hollow, a product of the last Ice Age, licked out
by the glacier's rasping tongue. More recent depths have certainly
been given the odd human helping hand, with rocks banked up at
the lip. All in all, it's a small but perfectly formed collaboration.

I try not to let my teeth clatter, as Roz bridles at nuisance
clouds, waits for the light, the right moment to click the shutter.
At last, she lets me go and I rise up, dripping like a pale leviathan,

anxious for the comfort of towel. As I turn to get changed, the sun has a burst of confidence. Dull green grass is gilded and the water glints, filled with glittering inclusions. The camera orders a repeat. Of course, I have to suffer for my art. And so I bend my knees and let the weight of bubbling water take me back. I try again to look nonchalant, wait for the click before I scream. What a wimp. Yes, I know there's a man who swims under arctic ice in a mere pair of trunks. Whoop-di-bloody-do. For me, this little water filled by a little fall, in a little batch, will do. I scramble out, the stream still suffusing me, the whole of the Long Mynd coursing through my body until it rings like a bell. The irritability that lay earlier like a lake between me and the world has been smoothed out, evaporated. God, I will miss my girl when she leaves home; my sweet Roz whose Barbie collection was once the marvel of the Western world, and whose stylish attire these days makes me look like a dowdy old git. However, today she is with me, sharing the moment, and I am content. My skin radiates, I am on fire and I shout like a loon, whooping to the hills. It's miraculous; the wonder of cold water, its ability to wipe clean worry and to launder dark thoughts.

I look over at my girl now sitting on a rock, writing as I get changed. Many winters ago, when Roz was still little, I went off on one of my solo dusk walks. A stillness had descended within the hedgerows lining the road – blackbirds, blue tits and the far rooks were settling down for the night. High above, two geese sought the last of the light, like arrows disappearing into water. I tramped through mud, seeking boundaries, far places on the edge of woods where the horizon gave onto distant hamlets hazed with woodsmoke, and single cars threaded the deep lanes like slow-moving lanterns. And there, as I peered over into the mess of hawthorn scrub, was an ancient bit of hedge and a glitter that caught my eye.

The dusk had been caught in a tiny pool not more than three inches across. I knelt down to inspect how it was done, marvelling at the combination of history and benign neglect. Back in the days when all hedges were cut by hand and not flailed with an oversized barber shop posing as a tractor, the bushes were taught through force, cutting, persuasion and forceful weaving to grow against their inclination. Sideways, in a drift, rather than towards the sun. Hence the great architectural wonder that is an old hedge. Over time, some of these branches thickened, so now there was a tree branch that had begun by growing horizontally from the trunk and then, once freed from the pernicious practices of laying, had sprung straight up. Where branch joined trunk, a natural hollow had formed and rain had done what it always does: pooling wherever it's contained.

There is a point to this. I couldn't swim in that tiny cruck-puddle, but I could take it away with me, the unwrapped present of that walk: a last gathering of reflection in a dim January dusk.

It was around this time that four-year-old Roz had trouble sleeping at night, whatever we did – milky drinks, calming mood music, cuddles, reassurance. Nothing worked until, one evening, that little pool of water came back into my head and turned into an adventure. I dislike the phrase 'guided meditation' but that's exactly what it was. A journey up into the woods in the company of a dragon and a mouse who happened to be best friends. There was one tree in particular that the adventurers headed for each night, a great old evergreen, hollow oak (somehow, leaves in winter were both important and hopeful). There were stairs carved around the girth. Even better, once up high, and where branch met trunk, a cosy cruck-pool was filled with steaming water. Yes, a naturally grown hot tub in the trees, safe, warm and reassuring. All this I told my daughter, and how once we had all (Dragon, Mousie, little Roz and me) swum and taken in the night view of the far Shropshire valleys and hills, then we found the door in the side of the tree. Beyond the door lay the warm bedroom, heated by sap where soft leaves provided the best mattress in the world.

It worked. A sleeping child was the tale's result, which later flew into the realms of one of my first picture books.

I blink my eyes, and the years, like Dragon, have flown past much too fast. It's time to leave. We pass Hanging Brink and Barrister's Batch and trudge up Sleekstonebank Hollow to gain the sky and see beyond the Mynd to the far plain of Shrewsbury and the North. The water below still sings, for here is another tributary of the Onny, the high-sprung place of its birth. I have explored many of these local rivers from tip to tail, until at last they leave the Borderlands swollen and pregnant with rain and a thousand beginnings. To say I know them would be an under-statement, but, after quarter of a century, we have come to an understanding. As my daughter strides alongside me, ready to wade out into the wide world, I also understand and am thankful that the day that extends before me right now is entirely different from the one I began this morning.

River Thames, Oxford

TODAY OUR CAR, PACKED TO ITS METAL RAFTERS, is broaching the borderland between childhood and adult. We carry Roz cross-country – our first baby, the girl I held in her first moments of new skin, new breath, new cries. On her first morning at home

I tucked her tiny smallness into a sling, zipped up my baggy green waterproof and ventured out into the high street of the small town we lived in. As I met neighbours and friends, the zip would fly down as I proudly showed off this papoosed miracle. I was bursting then and am still now, for all her hard work has got her here, to the city of Oxford, to a college that banks the River Cherwell.

I am pleased that water curves and curls past her halls of residence, that her room in a concrete Seventies building at least overlooks a huge fig tree, creating its own jungle canopy which shades her window. I try not to weep as Polly points out the food she has packed for her, and the moment of goodbyes awaits. It's easy to say she'll be back in nine weeks, but, suddenly, once again, I respect my own mother. I understand now what she went through when my brother and I left home. When I rang my mum last night, she told me about the day I too left home and how she had covered the living room with pictures of my brother and me, all that was left once we'd gone. I feel her tears now, as well as mine and those of Roz and Polly as I try to smile, reassure the little girl hiding inside the grown-up, kiss and hug goodbye.

My daughter and I have swum in sea, river, lake and waterfall. She has always understood that cold water is not necessarily a barrier, though she's drawn the line at wild-winter forays and hypothermic flirtation. She has grown up in nature and loves it still. Perhaps this is the best gift I can give her. When her grades were predicted and she began to think of university, I was wary of her applying to the place in which I had started out. What if my early academic failings at this selfsame university were somehow being channelled into daughterly expectation? But this was entirely her own dream, of her own work and making.

River Thames, Portmeadow

Bizarrely, when she was put out to the *pool* of other colleges – and I love the image which sums up the brutal sink-or-swim of endless interviews – she was interrogated by my old don. That particular meeting was curious as it seemed the professor was more interested in letting her know how much he knew rather than trying to elicit what *her* learning had achieved. I am glad (for my own sake) that this was not the college to have made her an offer, as the one that took her has a reputation for being welcoming. This is confirmed by the second-year student who takes us round and shows Roz her room and what's what. There is an understated calm friendliness here, perhaps mirrored by the river itself, its cool current soothing all those feverish synapses.

As we leave, we walk the bounds of the college to the soundtrack of piano playing, floating from an open window. There are old trees, gardens wilting gracefully into autumn and the thick green coil of the river roped round the edges. Then, our allotted parking time is up and we have to exit. It is tempting to drive straight home, to wander round my daughter's old room and to feel the full weight of eighteen years and the transition we uncertainly straddle. But that would be to miss all that the city has to offer.

Time for the condemned student's last lunch at a wonderful eatery in town. The food at Turl Street Kitchen is all prepared fresh, with a new menu every day depending on what's available. I have fresh crab on toast, with smoked salmon and pickled cucumber, Roz has salt cod croquettes with lemon aioli, and Polly the veg soup, all served with bread baked fresh that morning, still crusty and hot. In a country where it seems that some places charge you for actual crap on a plate, this family moment gilded by phenomenal food warms us thoroughly. The restaurant is packed for a reason – confirmed by the chocolate pecan nut tart washed down with loose-leaf tea made with mix of second flush Darjeeling and actual British-grown tea. We have sent our girl off with style and a feast, but sadly to a hall of residence where the 'kitchen' consists of a sink, fridge and microwave.

Suddenly, the car we parked earlier is empty of both stuff and the back-and-forth banter of years. It feels strange. I'm in need of open skies, and Port Meadow is the place to provide them. As we walk along the path and see the view open out, I am surprised all over again, having forgotten how vast this expanse is, a veritable Tardis of green, hidden by the city's boundaries. There are cows, and ahead of us a bridge, and lines of boats parked up on the Thames. Back when I was a student, I made friends with a musician called Pete Hall, who owned the boat that he lived on down here. His other work as a French polisher had stood him in good stead as his restoration and polishing of the teak-bound barque meant that it gleamed like amber. Pete played flamenco guitar and made me cups of vanilla tea and was a good father figure for a young man who had no father. He taught me you could live for art, whatever form that might take, and he has followed that dictum all his life. I have gratefully followed in his wake.

When the weight of Oxford cracked and broke above my head – when I also had the great fortune to meet a guru called Swami Shyam and to have been what I can only call indoctrinated by his acolytes – then, the beauty of this landscape turned ugly. I, who had sat with devotees eating mounds of overly sweet gulab jamun followed by hours of chanting; I, who had agreed that a guru eating a flower (a whole flower!) in front of his followers was indeed an experience of mind-blowing proportions; I, who had found myself wandering these very meadows, was crushed under the armour-plated pewter of sky. Looking back, it's pretty obvious that I was suffering from undiagnosed depression, not helped by being told I needed to meditate more and eat less produce from a chicken's bottom (i.e. eggs!). However, out of that loss, that inability to face exams, that sudden fear of outdoors, the abandoning of my course, I was soon ensconced in rehab, even though I was already clean and sober. My head was mush, and the no-nonsense therapy was an unexpected offering from the gods.

Out of failure, the sudden sad earth-fall which diverted the river of my ambition, I shed my academic self to become a poet and storyteller working with children in a new city: Bristol. A few years further on, and a storytelling visit to a school led to meeting a teacher called Polly, and further downstream, the inklings of love, and from that love, children. So, my last words to Roz were a statement of fact: that if I had not failed at Oxford, she would not be starting at Oxford!

Now, I'm walking in Port Meadow, on the banks of the river; lovely Polly is holding my hand and I'm trying not to cry. The cows and calves are still lives, clustered on the banks of the Thames, one black one a still darkness reflected in the water as she cools off under the sudden sun. It's hot, the early grey of day burned off. We walk and walk and I watch the water and the old homing instinct kicks in. What's that in my backpack? A just-in-case set of trunks and a small towel that Polly snorts is a hand cloth. We're too near the cattle, as indicated by the hoof marks, shit and squidge. So we keep going, in search of a better spot further upriver. We disturb a little egret, who gains the air and wings past, only the yellow of her eye disrupting the papery blankness of flight.

We find a shelving spot leading into shallow, clean-ish water. Perfect, though Polly is concerned that the towel I grabbed on my way out this morning will not cover my modesty to change, and gives me her jacket too. There are walkers, and an elderly couple seated on a bench on the far bank, but no one is bothered by a tall guy paddling out over soft mud that holds up well underfoot. I was expecting proper river coldness, but though I'm already up to my waist, I can still feel my toes. It's a good sign, as is the sun bouncing off this calm stretch of river. I know it's not wise to dive in, to get my head under water in case of 'things' lurking: viruses, microbes and such like. I know it with my head, but today, the heart's not listening. I have to commit. This is my water, my moment, and the Thames is the cleanest it's been for years. I've swum in it before, at Reading, in a mad young-twenties moment when WOMAD was freaking me out from sheer heat and numbers of people. The water did then what it does now as I point my arms like a plough and furrow under the landscape. I am mid-river, unable to feel the bottom, glad of no scary undertow or current. In fact, the river seems utterly still, as if it too has paused to admire the warm October afternoon. The far bank appears do-able, so I strike out, wait till I am close before slowly feeling for the rising shore. And there I am, on the other side of the Thames. For a brief moment I'm in the other far country we all dream of, looking back at my wife and thinking how good and right all things are.

I do feel that my body has changed, is continuing to change in response to wild swimming. Studies have shown that repeated cold-water swimming can alter the body's physiology. I don't know the science, but I do know we are adaptable. Each time I swim as it grows colder, I stretch far beyond the burn, ignore the shrill messages that say I am about to die, quell the panic in my bloodstream. From that point onwards, a delicious languor suffuses me. I step back in for the return crossing and, on the way back, I dawdle mid-river, treading water like a man kneading grapes into wine. For truly, I am drinking of this water-fuelled experience and today the sky no longer hangs threat-heavy as it did the last time I was here, but is the cap of thanks I doff to the gods.

On the way home, in the passenger seat, I catch up on the sleep I mislaid the night before. And though, when we unlock the house, I try not to go upstairs to look into Roz's room, it's easier said than done. The tears do come then, so strongly until there is no more sadness to heave up. We two parents hold each other and don't say anything. Thankfully, there is spaghetti bolognese to cook, our boy Asa to chat to and josh with, and change to be accepted for all that it brings.

Llyn Cau and Nant Cadair, Cadair Idris

WHEN I FIRST HEARD that my friend Seb had been diagnosed with a rare form of cancer that is particularly shit for men, I felt the shock we all do when presented with the bare facts of our mortality. All that could be well for him, was. He had family, children, worked hard, gave back to his community. Now this. How could I ever dare to complain about anything ever again? Instead, I did the best I could to be a mate, offered support when I could. But it was Seb who was rushed into surgery with no guarantee he'd survive. It felt entirely the wrong age to be contemplating the *what if* of leave-taking. His wife was left holding home and family together as we all wished and prayed for outcomes that seemed both uncertain and filled with statistical thinness.

The scalpel removed the cancer, and, in recovery, also metaphorically carved out his weight until Seb was more shadow than body. Yet within that dark corridor, the lamp still gave out

Cadair Idris

the glow that reflected the core of his spirit. He slowly got better, and better, and then some.

Today, we are driving to Cadair Idris, laden with fresh lemon tuna mayo sandwiches and a thermos of Brazilian coffee softened with hot milk. In the back, there is enough rope and bits with names I will soon be familiar with to get us up steep mountainsides. More importantly, in the driver's seat, Seb is so alive it's somewhat scary. When he pushed back from death, I think he made a decision that each of his days was precious. In the last two years alone, he has gained an amount of outdoor, wild-water, and climbing instruction skills that would normally take a decade to attain. All this alongside his day job, working with very challenging teenagers. Oh, and let's not forget the Open University engineering degree he's nearly finished, besides being a proactive member of his local community and a well-decent family man to his wife and four kids. I only have to look at Seb and I'm knackered.

Here's the thing. I dare, in our conversation, to parallel my experience of horrendous mental health with his own physical decline and then recovery. I almost feel that I should be ashamed of such a comparison. But that would be to give in to the 'pull-yourself-together' brigade, epitomised by the person who once asked Polly if she thought my getting slowly better might be to do with the weather. When I descended into that valley, I can say that death was as close as breath in my ear. Well, we both survived, Seb and me, and here we are, taking the piss out of each other, whooping in his old Beemer on the way into the vastness of high Wales.

I like the gods of late, the ones who, as we pull into the car park, down a track through dappled, yellowing trees, decide to draw the sun from behind the clouds, to conjure the very action of light that lifts every steep step up through the woods, following the rain-swollen Nant Cadair into the uplands. Seb jingles with all his gear, and the rope he has strapped to my back digs in with both weight and discomfort. I warn him that I am an expert at whingeing, but such is the view that opens out from this glacial glade, all complaints are rendered useless. Already, I am keen to get wet, as the pools that waterfall their way down the steep slopes beckon to me like silver naiads. But we are here for the climbing, with swimming to be the final gilding of the day.

Seb has not only gained himself an outdoor education, but he has also immersed himself in the landscape and its slow, glacial construction. He points to a rock bank that sits above us like a lopsided twenty-foot-high pillow. The stone appears to be filled with vertical grooves, gouged by a giant's fingernails. Striation. As the glacier moved, rock fragments and sand grains embedded in the base caused these extraordinary abrasions. The motionless structures are a snapshot of movement, now frozen in Welsh stone.

After two hours, we reach the plateau that contains the great north-facing lake of LLyn Cau, said to contain an *Afanc*, or water dragon, which was banished here by King Arthur. We skirt the edge of the lake until our target rocks are looming above us. Up until now, it's all been about joshing and japing. But as Seb sets out his stuff, puts me in harness and ties the rope that is theoretically supposed to help if I fall, the doubts set in. Even worse, after jabbering out a set of instructions that contain the words 'slack' and 'safe', Seb prances straight up the rock like a frigging mountain pony. Every so often, he stops to wedge in a piece of metal attached to looped wire called a 'nut'. Back in the early days of mountaineering, climbers used actual aluminium nuts from aeroplanes, threaded on a loop, to stick into crevices for anchoring purposes. The name has stuck, and within five minutes there is a Hansel and Gretel trail of them leading up towards the sky. Seb has vanished, and my job as second is to belay the rope that runs through my fingers on a device known as a 'grig'. At this moment, his life is in my hands. If he falls, we are tied together and, theoretically, my weight will stop him tumbling into the land of broken bones.

Two ravens drift past, almost within touching distance. We are not on any path now, and this route is not a well-known ascent. This is their country. Damn it, my camera is in my backpack, and their cronks are more of a sneering laugh. I hear a shout and panic. Wasn't he supposed to come back down and guide me up? I'm a novice. What do I do? Then it dawns on me. I'm supposed to climb now, taking out the 'nuts' as I go. I bellow out the action word 'Climbing!' and set off. The rock is not sheer. Indeed, this route is classed as 'Diff' for difficult. So, I am ten feet up before I realise what's going on. Suddenly, there are no convenient handholds, my boots appear pathetically ungrippy and I am supposed to find a way up this unholy wall to some out-of-sight mate who has abandoned me. Shit bloody shit. I find myself calling Seb a bunch of names my teenage son would approve of. There is no choice as the rope insistently tugs at me.

Of course, I know this place. It is a rock that lies ten feet above a waterfall; and the feeling is the same as the one I get when swimming in January, inching my feet towards the swirling water in front me; then, there is the commitment to sprint-swim into the middle of the lake while wondering if I will make it back before I freeze into splinters. This all seems a bit hard-man as I breathe, sweat, find a crevice for my hands, lever myself up – convinced that the tiny nothing on which my toe is balanced will let me down and that I will fall backwards into space.

But I don't fall, and that river of adrenaline soaking skin and soul has me hollering like a wolf as I reach the first rise. A few minutes later, I collapse at Seb's side and realise I have completed my first ever multi-pitch. My heart is racing and my vision sharpened. Like my son when I used to throw him in the air, my next word is 'More!'

We climb Cadair Idris, belaying, roped, anchored, creviced, straining muscles, paralleling a vertiginous waterfall, with us in reverse flow. The two ravens come back, float lazily in their element, skimming past us. I try to catch them on camera, but dark wings on an overcast day make for a hopeless picture. Higher still, there are peregrines screeching about the cliffs, their cries bouncing purely off the rock. Heather sprouts from every gap in the stone, a mix of incongruous purple when all around is subdued, and flowers browning into autumn.

Ninety minutes later, we've done it. I look back down at the dark mass of the brooding lake to see how far we've come. I could get into this. I have walked Cadair before, up the footpath like most ramblers do. This is more intimate, a sense of closeness to the mountain. We eat crisps and chocolate to celebrate, then half slip, half strain our way back down, bouldering the stream in spite of Seb's helpful comments that most accidents happen on the return journey. By the time we are level with the lake, my knees and calf muscles are very keen for the whole day to go away and leave them alone. The day, which started off warm, has dropped by a fair few degrees, so that the sweat on my skin instantly chills as I decide to skinny-dip. I show Seb how to use my camera, keen to get a record of myself immersed in the lake.

This, now, is the day's reward. I have swum Llyn y Gadair on the other side of the mountain after my last walking ascent. That was in a piping hot September and, theoretically, should have been fabulous. All I remember though is a numbing cold and a feeling that the lake was out to get me. I lasted only a few seconds as the acquaintances I walked with made killjoy comments. How easy it is to look on someone grabbing at life and disparage them while doing bugger-all yourself!

This afternoon feels utterly different. I dive in, letting clamminess and the day's efforts glide off my skin. The water is clean and smooth, reminding me of the time I drank from the stream that came off Rosenlaui glacier when I was young and my brother alive, and of mountain camping with Swiss cheese and yoghurt and the night-time cracking of the great ice walls thundering through my dreams. I swim through all those memories, out into the meltwater of many thousands of years, not worried about water dragons. All is view, openness, the whole valley now empty of walkers, and my nakedness entirely appropriate for this gift of Cadair. By the time I shoal myself out of the water, I am not sure if I actually have a pair of feet left at the end of my legs, and the wind reminds me I need to get togged up pretty bloody quickly.

I am fixed – and have had my fix – as we trail back down the contours, out of the afternoon, and find ourselves with rumbling stomachs when the kick of adrenaline wears off. But oh, the River Nant Cadair also looks like a bit of alright, and – what with the tiny tinge of sun that suddenly lights up a very inviting pool – I figure what the hell. Tiredness go hang. I must explore: one is too many and a thousand never enough. The second tingle of a skinny-dip feels different, though it is the same water, now in motion, in thrall to gravity's crooked tumbling rock finger. All is rush and bubble and swirl. It feels so good as I float, feet up in this supportive whirlpool, with no desire to get out. Tired muscles are soothed in the stream while a few rocks down a dipper shares my sense of joy. I am happy and we are done.

On the way home, we stop at the Cross Foxes Inn where it is my duty to treat my friend after a day where he was the gaffer, and I the clambering novice. Obviously, hearty hunger makes most food taste good. But this is magnificent, the perfect chapter ending to a day that contains two of its own miracles: Seb and myself both living to tell the tale, and those few hours of reaching up within touching distance of the sky.

River Teme, Leintwardine

LAST NIGHT, I TREKKED OFF to hear a talk given by acclaimed wildlife photographer Mark Sisson. To commemorate fifty years of work, Shropshire Wildlife Trust has commissioned a book by Mark, celebrating what this county has to offer. Mark's talk was both an insight into what he does and a ravishing PowerPoint presentation of his photos. Here is a man whose understanding of water I now fully admire, alongside his dedication to getting the perfect shot. He spent one whole summer building a relationship with a pair of great crested grebes, which were nesting on a lake in the middle of Telford town centre. The water in those images reflects the housing estate that butts up to the banks of the lake. And among the discarded bottles and rubbish that we humans strew to reflect the fact that some of us really don't give much of a damn, there is new life hatching out.

Mark's work is all about the eye-level picture, which requires great patience and slowness. Taking this sort of photo is perhaps

In the field behind my house

the opposite of wild swimming with its joyous leaping and thrashing exit once the cold bites. His entrance into the lake, togged up in chest-high neoprene waders, requires calmness, not frightening the birds that have slowly, over months, got used to him. Even his tripod ends up submerged, until his camera and lens are no more than an inch above water. The results are worth it – such as his shot of an egg emerging from a female water bird, a picture that took twenty years to capture. Later in his sequence, the chick takes its first floating ride out into the wide world of the lake, tucked under the mother's wing feathers. When I think of the hours, days, months it has taken him to achieve this series of pictures and tell the story, I admire his commitment, and my own photography suddenly feels inadequate.

Mark was friendly after his presentation and happy to share some tips: tips I am armed with this dawn as I creep through the field behind my house. The forecast has shown a rare break in October's grey and the sunrise shows potential. However, it's not the lightening skies I am after, but hare – that skittish, beautiful symbol of all I hold dear in this county and country. From numbering four million in the late 1800s, the decline of the hare has been scary and predictable, with numbers down 80 per cent. In Shropshire, we are lucky to have them still and there are always a few to be spotted by those with patience and stealth in the hills around my village.

What this experienced photographer has pointed out suddenly makes sense. As I trudge towards a spot where I know that hares like to hang out, one of them ups from the brown mud and accelerates away in the pre-sunrise gloom. My camera would not stand a chance, especially as hares can achieve speeds up to forty-five miles an hour. Dammit. I think I've spoiled my chances already, galumphing amateur that I am. I might as well give up and go home. But what is that lighter brown smudge on the edge of the ploughed soil? I focus, snap off an image and the blurred result confirms it. Hares are not like rabbits, which dig burrows. They prefer to scrape out shallow depressions in the ground called forms, and flatten down into them, ears back – exactly like this one is doing now. I follow Mark's instructions. I drop down, creep with knees bent, telling this hare over and over that I am no threat. It seems to work. My lowered body presents no silhouette, giving me a greater chance. There is no sudden bolt, no fur rocket streaming into the distance, and within a few minutes I am only yards away, though I am not willing to wriggle on my belly yet. Perhaps that is for another time, for I am close enough now. All I have to pray for is the rising of the light. No tripod, so I improvise with a fence post and some tissues from my pocket, balance the lens and use the touch screen to focus and snap.

So here is Hare, standing, preening, licking his front legs and using them to rub and wash his face. As the sun breaks through, I have him against a backdrop of scraggy hawthorn and dried-out grasses – the catchlight of his bright eye, the rich brown of his fur, the crazy length of his ears streamlined back against his body as he comfortably settles in his form at the top of the field. I have stayed still for so long that a grey squirrel is picking up hazelnuts within three feet of me and the far-off buzzard begins to criss-cross the woods behind, assured by my unmoving weight. Gratitude wells for all this that I haven't created but simply chanced upon through deciding to rise early.

The day holds yet more gifts. The rains have receded, leaving roads polished and shiny, and a zing in the air. I have to collect some of my photos from a framer this afternoon in Leintwardine. His expert mounting has brought to life my water shots of both the rural Borderlands and the more urban flow of cities. I am obsessed with London by night, and all things and buildings Thames-related. Having swum its upper reaches, I know that the river around Tower Bridge, Big Ben and the Shard is best left for the birds. Undercurrents and eddying whirlpools round bridge buttresses are entirely dangerous for tiny, puny humans.

Yes, David Walliams did swim the whole length of the Thames for charity (and was made ill by it) and yes, he is therefore brave and even more crazy than me. But he and the salmon are welcome to this brown murk of declivity. Yet by night, over long exposure, sky and water interchange and the Thames becomes the blue of lapis lazuli, the rich burnish of medieval jewellery. Buildings become backdrop against a hued landscape, a single wash that means I am still swimming in it as I take my pictures.

After my frames are wrapped and packed into bright green bubble wrap and safe in the boot of my car, I drive to the bridge over the River Teme and park under an ancient oak still holding on to its leaves. The temperature is ridiculous, T-shirtable even, this late in October. In midsummer, the common next to the river on the edge of town is awash with teenagers and walkers, and birders out to spot the sand martins that nest in the banks. A busy place that I usually avoid when I'm in search of a solitary, soulful dip. We're out of season now though. The vast common, containing the oxbow meandering of the Teme, is empty except for a distant hawk, the glitz of sun acting on water and a few gardeners out preparing their plots for winter on the other side of the river. In my other, doppelgänger life, I have often imagined moving into one of the houses here, a New England-style wood-framed structure that sits prettily and cleanly on its perch overlooking the river. It seems like a good life – the one I place myself in, like a paper cut-out – though I would swap secateurs for trunks, build a pontoon out into the depths and then dip every day come sun, snow or rain. Ever since Grahame's Ratty burst upon the literary world, alongside Jerome's three men in a boat, there must have been so many of us who harbour a hidden river-dweller deep inside our psyches.

House envy will get me nowhere. For I claim the river as mine this early afternoon and hop down from the eroded bank onto a smooth pebble beach to get changed. I like smooth rocks, the fact that sometimes the action of time and water do my feet favours. Welsh mountain rivers are often all about sharpness and hidden spikes of quartz or granite. This mellow entry into the Teme is rolling Shropshire all over. I decide not to tarry, but dive, ignoring that old warning bell tolling in my head.

I swim downstream in a water not yet packed with winter's chill, the whole of the Teme belonging to me on this quiet afternoon. I think back to our honeymoon in the South of France, and the day we boulder-trekked a deep gorge river. The road clinging to the valley a few hundred feet above us was narrow to the point of despair, and it was very odd to shallow-dive into the water to find a windowless shell of a car calmly wedged in the clear flow just beneath my flailing feet. It seemed pretty obvious that whoever had fallen that far in their car would not have survived the unintended swim. The discovery brought disquiet to our river experience – that this beautiful stretch was the probable scene of so much grief – and there was a strange uneasiness to the whole area because of it.

The Teme holds no such rusting shocks as I breast-stroke towards a weeping willow out in the deeper reaches, swim through its still leafy fronds, finally feel the burn in my body, and turn to accelerate towards the shore. Climbing out, I turn to look at the colour of the Teme and see that I've definitely broken my post-rain, no-swim rule. The level of the water is up, its mud colour indicating field run-off, silt from further up and who knows what delight of fertilising or pesticidal wonders. My skin should already be feeling that familiar, over-sensitive itch to indicate that the water is not entirely natural. However, the signals of my body-barometer to impurities in the water are surprisingly reassuring on this gentle afternoon. My skin merely feels clean, and I dive in again to savour every part of the river, which, like Mark Sisson, I am now experiencing at eye level, and trying to frame through the apparatus of words and the shutter of simile.

I grin as I change, crazy-glad, mad-happy for a day that began with a hare and ended up here.

Lydbury at dawn

november

Rhaeadr Du Waterfall

Rhaeadr Du Waterfall, Wales

THE RAIN HAS BEEN UNCEASING, a battering ram of silver stair rods as all the heavens march down. Last night, we lay cradled in our carved-out loft bedroom, far too near the slate roof of this former chapel, and I wondered if our once holy home would withstand the storm. But nobody and nothing messes with good Welsh slate. Truly, it was water off a cruck's back.

Today, the emptying of the sky has done all our moods a favour. There is light once more and we're rejoicing in it. Even better, a chore is taking me over towards Marshbrook and Church Stretton, and my prior scrutiny of the map has revealed two lakes that look promising, with the added bonus that they are near enough to a footpath to mean I'm unlikely to be shot by a pheasant-guarding gamekeeper. I tell Polly I might be some time and set off into the afternoon, driving past the old train station of Plowden that last saw service in 1935, then climbing the east flank of the Long Mynd before dropping down towards the A49 and a wood I have never once visited, despite it being twenty minutes from our house.

I love how trees are able to enclose unto themselves, to fold up the roar of traffic into a soft, forest-carpeted hush. The conifers wear a wealth of dark shadows and promise hidden liquid delights. I decide to bushwhack and feel a sense of ridiculous jungle-daring in my thirty-foot scramble through bramble, fern and dying nettle, all the time seeking the trickling source that tickles the ear, or the eye-hook of smidgens of far silver. With all that rain, I am walking through bog land. Just there, through scratchy bush at the end of a path that did not exist until I made it, lies my gilded grail: a pool hollowed in the scoop of the stream.

A puddle of a sorry, unloved affair, it is more drip than lake, with all the swim potential of a blocked sink. All I can do is look on in sorrow, turn and retreat.

Never mind, I am committed to this day, this light, this sky that insists on a swim. The map shows me bigger prey in the form of Soudley Pool. Surely, with all that pale, printed cyan to indicate water, there will be a welcome for me there? But, despite the clearing out of clouds, and the lone buzzard that rears up out of the abandoned orchard, where the twisted apple trees have been forgotten like relatives in a sepia-tinted photograph, my glimpse of the lake is just that. Barring my way to the water, rearing like a checkpoint border wall of separation, is a barrier of chicken wire at least eight feet high. Is this to stop the desperate pheasants from fouling the water? Mind you, the green scum that covers the lake hardly looks inviting, and the single swan in residence flies straight towards me as if to say he was hired to guard against invaders. The 'Private' signs appear to have been breeding and I decide, wisely, that Soudley Pool needs to be left to its own devices.

That could be my day done, but I have come for a dip and I don't divert so easily. On the way back, I stop at an old favourite pull-in. The Long Mynd plateau rears its ferny flanks on one side, with a farmhouse tucked into the cleft at the bottom quite tidily. On the other side, the valley of the Onny wends its way towards the town of Craven Arms. There is a gate to slip through and a farm track that drops towards an old ford in the river, beyond which it curves into depth and the sites of many years of family summer visits. In fact, this spot dates even further back in our shared history, as Polly's mother discovered it was the ideal place to walk her dog in the Eighties. At eighteen, Polly used to come here with her friends to drink wine on hot afternoons and picnic time away.

Today, the river looks wrong for swimming but for once I won't listen to the evidence, despite the fact that contours and levels have been dissolved. All is caramel, crush and rush, whisk and boil as transformed rain hurries in its cycle to the sea, to be heaved up by heat again in the great chirruping round robin of all things circular and magnificent. My rule, as mentioned before, is simple: if it's thick-brown, you drown. But, I figure, the water's fairly shallow here, barely knee height. This is not Ludlow, where the floods turn the Teme into a horizontal wall of charged acceleration. I must have water to wash away the failure of those previous pools.

I change and step gingerly. The shallows where dippers usually bob over the stones are deeper than I was expecting. They have been replaced with a current that *should* be no threat. But already, I feel the weight of water, and can work out that if I move only a couple of feet to my right, I will not be able to stay upright. I study the surface of the Onny like a wily angler, calculate the place of stillness, where speed and surge skirt round but not into. I spot it and sink into that brown movement and moment; feel myself slipping even as I scrabble upwards again, alive to the danger. The river is a beast that I do not know today, as if the circus lion I have worked with for twenty years suddenly had a sniff of savannah, or smelled the cut on my finger and decided that friend was indeed edible. Trust has gone. The river has its own mind and gravity is its dictator. To fight it would be foolhardy, and so this becomes the shortest of dips in a day that has not quite satisfied, but which has left something unfinished and undone.

•   •   •

It isn't until I head to Barmouth with my wife and son for the half-term holidays that I feel able to complete what I started.

We live in a land that surges and swells with water, whose rivers sometimes contain antiques and hints of history. For instance, at Oakleymill Waterfall in my home county of Shropshire, the mill has left only its name behind; yet, with all that power for free, watermills once existed all over the country, seven of them bridging the River Fleet in London to grind the corn for London's bread. Instead, today, all around us, the energy companies are laughing all the way to their shareholders' meetings while they stiff us with above-inflation rises. We complain about the rain, but don't harness it much any more.

Maentwrog Power Station in Wales is an honourable exception and a feat of engineering that takes gravity and water-flow to turn them into thirty megawatts of lights, toasters and computers. From darkness, water carries light. The river powering it is the Afon Prysor, which falls through the Woodland Trust site of Coed Felinrhyd.

On this light November morning, we skirt the edge of the power station and play follow-my-leader in reverse with the river. We are quickly enveloped in a green-hued world. Yes, the leaves are beginning to turn, engaged in the yearly migration from vibrant saturation to fallen, faded compost. But the trees themselves are green, brave old sessile oaks that have survived simply due to the luck of geography, for who can farm or graze such deep valleys?

Strands of silky swan-neck moss bend in the breeze. This verdant, coated lushness has no prejudice, happy to spread from bark to rock and back to bark again. How amazing that it reproduces vegetatively. Bits break off and become new life. Sex by falling apart. There are feather mosses and flapworts, and some of the lichens that paint this forest are known by Hornby enthusiasts the world over, their miniature bushiness the landscape around which a thousand attic railways ran.

This is the damp, humid, moisture-laden jungle we climb through, the glacial river below still carving out ever deeper cuts and drops in the rocky land. Half an hour later, the sound of the falls still accompanies us. It is the rumbling, hissing hum of water. Growing up in London, I always slept with my window open and found the soft murmurations of distant traffic, even the sudden screech of brakes, strangely comforting. But a river is a lullaby in motion and today it cradles the promise of my day's goal. A steep, cleared scuffle of undergrowth on the left indicates the route down to the falls. Everywhere is treachery, with leaves that delivered summer now offering the slimy potential to break ankle and leg.

We have to grab hold of lower branches, of rocks, of anything that will stop us careering down, until at last we come out onto a naturally shelving pebble beach. I am no Livingstone, cannot claim to be the first person here – the charred fire pit to my right indicates that in summer it's a place much visited. But this afternoon, where we have met no one on our little trek, the falls of Rhaeadr Du belong to us. The pool is enormous, a giant forty-foot supplicant's begging dish for the constant stream of rice that pours from above. Truly, we are in a Welsh Eden. This is clean water, brown and clear, not bothered by the recent flummox of rain. No silt, no pesticide, no brown foam, no flood of fear, only the funnelling of the high mountains trammelled in this curving corridor.

I change and don't dally, except to give Polly my camera with instructions to shoot the swimmer if he misbehaves. Then I dive in, swim towards that white rush, feel the force of the water spilling onto and over me as I let the pull of the current veer me out of the depths and back to the shallows. All joy is mine, except for the fact that I had set up the camera for a two-second delay, which I don't realise until I climb out. It has to be reset, and means I have to go back in. I'm really not complaining though – who would when repetition is just more of a good thing? Yes, the water is starting to take on the month's qualities, the chill that is not yet a threat, more a hint. But the exhilaration is entire, a defiant snub in the face of winter. *This* is exactly the swim I've been craving since my last, failed attempts. Yah boo to darkness.

The eloquence of Edward Thomas sings its way into my mind. He wrote: '...the summer is gone. The midnight rain buries it away where it has buried all sound but its own.' True, but all that rain is a transformation that makes this Welsh waterfall spring to life. Though summer has truly gone, something new arises and I have found it here, as I drip and dry off on the smooth, water-worn pebble beach.

I'm also grateful to other wild swimmers who wrote about this place and guided me here; they are my motion-filled mentors. There was no entrance fee, no sign to warn me I might die, no 'Private' placards. All I had to do to earn this delight was to walk and to scramble and to offer up willingness to step beyond unsatisfying dips and dive into the great thundering falls of Rhaeadr Du.

Rutland Water, Rutland

POLLY HELD OUT THE PHONE TOWARDS ME. 'It's the police,' she said as my heart began hiccupping. Even more strange, the sergeant was calling from a police station in Bedford. I wondered if I had possibly committed a murder that had somehow slipped my memory. Instead, the voice on the line told me that one of our poetry books had done the rounds of the building and everyone loved it. Then it became clear. They were referring to my and Polly's collection for teenagers, *Poems With Attitude*, now sadly assigned to that out-of-print cemetery in the sky. But this was over twelve years ago, when the book was still selling well, with its themes covering drink, drugs, relationships, friendships, family, bullying and all the recognisable stuff that is the discoloured glue of British society. The words were honest and it appeared that the poems had even reached into the heart of the Bedfordshire police force.

They were so impressed, they decided to set up a day in a school, with me performing and running a workshop. I have no issue with taking on two hundred thirteen-year-olds and enjoy the balance of entertaining and provoking thought for an hour. Most young people respect honesty, and brushing-under-the-carpet is not in my nature. So, I told them about my father's suicide, my heroin-addicted brother who later died of AIDS and my own whirlpool of addiction from which I had been fortunate enough to swim free.

In the Q and A session afterwards, once the kids had asked about the details of every single drug I had ever taken, one too-clever-for-his-own-good boy wondered whether I broke any laws these days, and what was the naughtiest thing I had done

Rutland Water

recently. As it happened, the night before, I had been driving south on the M1 and realised that police hospitality extended only so far. I was staying in the luxury of a service station hotel, a place where architecture had fled for the hills. Wildlife in this concrete landscape consisted of lesser spotted chocolate wrappers huddling in the corner of brick canyons. So I was in need of greenery, air, light, water, especially as the sunset was glorious

– all of England opening up under bright canopies and the grey afternoon smudged into memory.

This was, of course, in pre-Sat Nav days, that barbaric era when we relied on pieces of paper called maps in large books called road atlases. There was a blue patch indicated on the next exit, which felt like a promise. So I hightailed it out of that service station and found the exit, used my nose to guide me on smaller roads and then located a place to drop my car. What I was looking for, along the edges of what was obviously not a public lake, was access. We humans are wily and ingenious. Fishermen will always find a way to water, beat a path, circumnavigate fences.

There it was, a dark hollow, filled with bent-back branches and trodden nettles. I followed the last of the light until I came to a leaf-strewn shore where the hidden shining revealed itself. The end of the day had gathered all its luminous energy and laid it to rest on the undulating flatness before me, right there, right then. I changed and waded in, all those acres briefly mine even though just beyond the belted trees, huge industrial flatlands spread their manufactured wings. A few coots kept to reedy edges, their creamy white beaks catching the last of the light. A far-off swan beat out a thrum of wings, slapping the water in annoyance, pushing off from the viscous surface to gain the sky. I, meanwhile, gained the water, the coolness of it, the late-summer promise, the coat that would cover my dreams that night.

So here's my point. In answer, I told the pupil at the school the next day about my naughty bit of possible trespass, thinking the many ranks of police in the back row would be amused, would shrug their shoulders at my eccentricity. But I swear that was the moment some of the adults in uniform found the poet's pill too bitter for their liking. They bristled. It was agreed later that I had indeed delivered a strong, thought-provoking session and had offered a very moral stance regarding drugs and their dangers. Swimming wasn't mentioned, though I wasn't ever invited back. It's not a swim I regret, though, and even now as I think about it, I am back in that semi-urban wilderness, humbly receiving all that the water offered that day.

Today, so many years later, the sun is bright and clear. I wake in a well-proportioned eighteenth-century room, in an empty off-season hotel. I am the only guest, getting ready for an author visit in a school up the road. I dine well – local poached eggs, crisp bacon, my own Darjeeling tea. Last night, I sat by the fire and ate a phenomenal pizza and homemade pecan nut ice cream. Food lovers flock to the Fox and Hounds in Exton, Rutland, for the chef was a baker first and it shows in his cooking. The village, like most round here, is principally built of stone that is so honey-coloured it makes me peckish. Having eaten, I wish to feast on what lies in the valley below.

I've been to Rutland Water once before. That time, the water was merely the underling of sky, a grey froth-whipped uninviting custard. Even a hardened swimmer like me baulked at the opportunity. But the sun has performed a makeover most successfully. The great, meandering bulk of the lake is utterly transformed and not even the bully-bite of a harsh November wind can deter me. I park, prepare my camera with filters and polarisers that take colour and melt it in the furnace. I am layered up against the cold and, as I approach the shore, I see the level of the lake has dropped so that, despite no path, I can make my way along.

The evidence that Rutland is man-made lies before me. At the water's edge strewn stumps of trees shine like the stark, sawn-off, Roman remnants of an empire long gone into ghostliness. Their long-gone leaves are no more than a wet whisper. I look for the perfect spot, as contours curve round. Behind a copse of willow, still hanging on to their leaves, a natural bay reveals itself. The wind sighs once, then dies, beaten by simple geography. The birds have arrived here before me: goldeneye with their lovely white patches under their bright yellow eyes, and tufted ducks sporting curved tuft-extensions on their heads that would be fashionable on the catwalks. They settle on the breeze-free waters of this natural harbour. As ever, and I try not to take it personally, by the time I have got my infernal new zoom to do its job, they've gone, un-snapped except for the odd blur on my screen.

Never mind, I'm here for other reasons. I lay down my waterproof and change into my trunks. It's almost warm in this sheltered spot, but once I'm out on the lake, I know that the trees can no longer protect me. Ah well. This is it then. At least the shore is fairly compacted clay. No sludge to sink into, nor stones to catch on toes. And, let me assure you, November has finally taken its toll. Whatever remnants of summer lay suspended in these vast bodies of water are long gone. I push long slow strokes out into Rutland Water, ignore the fear of the very hugeness of it. It's mad, and wonderful. The place is empty. There might be a few dog-walkers nearby, or the odd birder with binoculars trained on the surface; however, I can see no one and nothing. Being alone has never felt so fantastic. For I am in the actual lake, swimming despite the imminence of winter, despite the horrible cold I have been fighting for days. And this water, this gigantic clay-coloured field ploughed with inland waves, is for this instant all that holds me on the earth.

My legs are numb, my toes no longer attached to my body. This is no extended swim, but more of a darting-in-and-out. I scramble to shore, feel the goodness of the world as I run from the wind into the little forest sunspot where the trees are friendly, holding up limbs to cover my cold skin. How is it that the timing of these jaunts feels sacred? The moment I've changed, clouds roll in, morning light gone in a drifting cover-up, sun already submerged and not coming back up for air.

Later, before I begin my performance to a rather large group of twelve-year-olds, the teacher introducing me asks the pupils what is the maddest thing they can think of that the author Andrew Fusek Peters has actually done that morning. Without a guiding clue, a boy puts up his hand and says, 'Swim in Rutland Water!'

Bog Pool, the Long Mynd

'All the clouds that lowered upon our house.'

Shakespeare, *Richard III*

WHAT IS THE DARKNESS that pushes down on us like pressed leaves? My friend H has careered in and out of depression. At the moment, the outside world is, for her, an accusation she cannot defend herself against. I write her a card, trying in my heart to let her know she is not alone. As I mentioned earlier, through the short months of last year, my house became Plato's cave, the sofa a jail I was in no way equipped to escape from. The rare times I was persuaded to leave the house, wind and the fox of cold that nipped at my neck were nothing better than torture. What could be easier than driving to the local indoor heated pool with my son for a half hour of lengths and larking about? But such was the grip on my mind of this debilitating illness, even the distance between my parked car and the

Bog Pool, Long Mynd

leisure centre became a marathon of endurance as I stuck with the friction of fear on the front seat, shivering as though winter lay within me.

The worst thing was that I was conscious throughout, like a patient aware of incisions and the surgeon's taut deliberations. So, the shame of it cut into me, my attempts at fatherhood botched between the changing room and the pool. I couldn't do it.

My son pretended all was normal when it wasn't, and my friend Soma gently tried to coax me into the water; me then as skinny as the beanpole that was my nickname at school. Her patience was like the water itself, without boundary, spilling over from who I had been before, to the person in front of her, so self-consciously dis-abled. I found immersion excruciating, I who had dived into Welsh waterfalls in winter without a second's hesitation. But I was a changeling, a stand-in substituting for the man I had been. I stood waist deep in the shallow end while my friends dunked and splashed my son and gave him all the fathering I could not even approximate. This was Andrew as bystander, audience, watcher of the world's going on. And I remember every single minute of it clear as the spring I have often drunk from high in the hills above Barmouth.

My relationship with water had become dysfunctional, and stayed that way for many months, with occasional forays into local, heated swimming pools where I managed fifteen minutes tops until the safety of the hot shower. How could such change happen, creep up on me unawares? And what is this identity that seems so fluid, so dictated to by the gravity of emotion where character ebbs and flows, and where the years that fix us into routines sometimes spill over? Banks are broken, and the deluge of denial is utter and complete.

The miracle is that I am sitting writing on the same sofa I was so recently anchored to; but time is a river that has looped, meandered and used its mouth to dig out a new channel. Within that current of many months has come healing, and a different sort of day, which began with my delving into my Landranger map, searching for the blue hollows, and the promise of what they contain.

I'll admit that sunshine helps to ameliorate the November chill. There is an anticipatory thrill hovering at the edge of my veins. We have food packed, warm clothes and a car to carry us into the hill. My son is going on a different journey today, old enough to stay home. Bizarrely for a thirteen-year-old, he is keen to tidy his room and do his homework. It's all preparation for tomorrow's adventures, when his friend will come over and they'll set sail on a new film that begins with flip-cameras and ends in the laptop editing suite and YouTube. His independence is a thing to behold, again the sense of change flowing through our family.

The road we take is one of the steepest in the Borderlands. We pass the ancient train station of Plowden, now a house; the bank that runs into the trees all that remains of the South Shropshire railway. The car then hugs the skirts of the Long Mynd, the great ridged whale that lowers over the flat plains of Shrewsbury beyond. Then we are heading up the single-track, pockmarked tarmac, trying to ignore the vertiginous descent on our left. It's funny how the mind still plays tricks. One tweak of the steering wheel and our car would be trying to imitate the gliders that hover over the landscape, trying to imitate birds as they catch the thermals and updrafts.

The echoes of my depression are still just beyond earshot. They persist in my mind's insistence that, however good it is now, these glory days of wild swimming, of laughter, of family, of the flowering creativity that blossoms into my laptop, all this will be taken away. 'All shall be ill and all manner of things shall be ill' seems to be the mantra. It takes an awful lot of CBT to change the tape. So one thing I do is to focus on the landscape around me, the perfect now of its sensation, colours, the last flare and fizz of the trees where every branch dreams of fireworks.

This intense study of leaf and tree, bird and sky that bears each wing aloft brought similar release to the poet Edward Thomas, for whom depression was both friend and foe. Sometimes, he would walk all night, perhaps trying to outpace his demons; his books such as *The South Country* and *The Icknield Way* have been Bibles to me, their words promising that there is more to this life. I have often cleaved to his writing, used Thomas as my before-bed prescription, the river I dive into, whose current I trust to carry me to some measure of peace and – when depression no longer holds a crooked sway – to sleep.

These lines from Thomas's poem 'The Mill-Water', about a disused watermill, bring their own elegiac comfort:

> Sometimes a thought is drowned
>
> By it, sometimes
>
> Out of it climbs;
>
> All thoughts begin or end upon this sound,
>
> Only the idle foam
>
> Of water falling
>
> Changelessly calling,
>
> Where once men had a work-place and a home.

On the very top of the Long Mynd, there is a strange square of trees, standing like sentinels around a barbed wire fence. Within, only mounds and grass, but on the map the name Pole Cottage, home of the gamekeeper. I have a photo from way back, showing dead pheasants laid out front of a dwelling, history reduced to a blur of black and white, revealing what is now just echo.

We park and begin the search for wild water that the map insisted exists. The land is tufted here, bog and heath and peat all cobbled together to make snares for ankles. Such level ground holds its secrets well. So well, that we come upon the small lake before we even know it, a spreading of thick blackness held within this lip of high land.

'It's November,' the voice of sense whispers in my ear. But I have long learned to disregard those whispers. Whatever the season, this is now my irregular, lopsided pool, puckered by the soft drizzle that sucks sound from the landscape.

Many years back, I presented a TV feature on the Long Mynd ridge in Shropshire, delved into its history, loved the fact it was once sea-bound and that often one crunches the fossils of long-gone shell-suited swimmers underfoot. I'd had the bright idea of introducing the piece with a surfboard. The camera crew went one step further, insisting I wear trunks to make my historical point. Needless to say, it was a freezing February morning. And I had to stand with the eight-foot board in nothing but my briefs while the cameraman insisted that every take wasn't quite right, later pissing himself laughing with the soundman over my near frostbitten experience.

A pair of brown plover burst from the foot-high forest of heather, chirruping with indignation at this gatecrasher. A bank of cloud, washed in taut electric grey, hovers above me, containing the threat of storm. I change and wade in through the soft squish of decomposed leaves. Apart from the standard shock, I am surprised at the cleanness of this shallow lake, the silkiness that drapes around my body. I manage to strike out, breast-stroke across the unreflecting black pool, where the view around me is a good forty miles in each direction and Hay Bluff is a downtown stroke on the horizon. I am subsumed in the dark browns of November – reed, mud and fallen leaves. In different seasons, this little pool shines with the lightness of a saturated sky. Not today, when reflections are cancelled and darkness folds around me. I'm not complaining, for every month has its merit and even the fact of my being out here now contains its own delight. I am happy to be the slow ranger, a wading bird come home to roost in the high marchlands.

Because of the view, the pool expands to a vast circumference. I am swimming not in a ridge-top bog, but actually navigating this landscape, forging and furrowing my own fluid dreamlines, connecting with the Shropshire that was and is now; the me that was so terrified, filled with faith once again. Here, water is transubstantiated into fine feeling and the shock of the new wakes me to the glories of life again. And again.

december

Mine-shaft swim

Semi-submerged Mine Shaft,
South Shropshire

GOOGLE HAS LED ME to this improvised car park on the edge of the woods, where a bunch of burly men are dry-suiting up under the light of their head-torches. But that was merely navigation: the true prompting that sees me stripping to cold-pimpled flesh and dragging my pathetic summer wetsuit over my skin was an open day at this mine three months ago. I delved then into the underworld of these lead-barium veins, accompanied by families and a safety-conscious guide, also called Andy, who dutifully pointed out low ceilings. All dug by pickaxe and dynamite, valuable seams of galena followed deep into the hills.

I wondered aloud if there might be a water connection and my wondering is what got me here tonight, among this gang who generally meet up once a week. I love the hobbies of the British. These four guys, all members of the Shropshire Mining and Caving Club, like to differentiate themselves from other cavers, as they are all about exploring industrial artefacts and man-made incursions into the underworld. Lamps are checked, my hard hat fitted, and Ian, the cameraman, sorts out his waterproof boxes before we set off into the dark. Bizarrely, there are two Andys in the group besides myself.

We skirt a reservoir and start following the criss-cross of old industrial paths, now covered in beech leaves, higher into the heart of forgotten industry. Beneath our feet, rusty Victorian pipe-work betrays the efforts that men undertook to lower the water table deep underground and pump out the excess, which has created the pool that now lies ten minutes behind us.

Of course, the industry that reshaped this landscape has long gone. The water has returned from both spring and hill run-off to fill 450 vertical feet of davits, shafts and adits. The place of drowned ghosts. As we walk through the woods and I try to make small talk, I also try not to think that I shall soon be burrowing down with these strange gentlemen. This is what I pitched for, when I threw out the idea of subterranean swimming to Ian and asked if these Borderlands held any down-deep rivers. His answer has brought us here, in a night when torchlight catches the mist from our breath and the leaves crunch under my wellies.

There it is. A barbed wire fence with a small gap underneath that looks as uninviting as possible. In size and shape, the mine entrance resembles a badger sett, with a tiny spoil heap of scree. The entry technique is simple. A feet-first slide and squeeze out of the land of moss, fern, lichen, fallen piles of leaves, into a tunnel where suddenly the world is not below my feet, not something I straddle or stride over, but is inches above my head, a pickaxed ceiling streaked with the constant percolation of water. Then I am through, my wellies splashing, the lights from my helmet picking out an impossible river receding into the cut-rock infinity. The other undergrounders have let me go first, as bodies in water will disturb the long-settled sediment, turn this see-through liquid luminescence into a swirling iron-rich fudge.

My months of cajoling the club have paid off. I wade into waist-high five-degree water, glad of all-over neoprene as I bow down, almost in homage to this underworld shrine; and then I am breast-stroking down a crystal channel, unable to believe the grace of my luck even as that particular clarity trickles down my neck and into my shoes, to remind me I am here not thanks to evolution but thanks to man and dynamite and history.

The only sound apart from my breathing and the splosh of my body is the constant drip of water permeating these rock formations, known as the Mytton Flags. Water is both persistent and consistent. It will find its own level without pumping, which is why this shaft will always stay semi-submerged and is, theoretically, safe. Floods due to heavy rains are cave events. Even were there to be two weeks of solid rain, the level in this swimming hole would not rise by more than a couple of inches. It's the same with the temperature: a constant five degrees all year round. Here is stasis, interrupted only by my clumsy progress.

My torch picks out streaks of quartz and calcite running like crazy-paving over the roof. Fifty yards in, it appears the tunnel simply ends, filled with a mound of grey mud and stone except for a tiny gap over to the left below the roof. Rock fall? Shaft collapse? Nothing about this is inviting. What if it happens again? Cradled in the belly of this rocky beast, were there to be a seismic shift, a geological abruptness, we would be no more, buried, never to come out.

No point moithering. One of the other Andys, blessed with a bit more girth and a dry-suit to keep him warm, has already worked his way through. He assures me that the method is simple. Arms out front, and wriggle. Perhaps this is the moment to back out.

However, he-man instinct and pride have a lot to answer for. There is also within me a tiny growing spark of insane bravery. I mostly sit at a desk to make a living these days, but wild swimming edges me off the shores of safety. My spirit needs the fire of risk to breathe and it beats those hours I spent watching 'Antiques Sodding Road Trip' on television when I was mentally stuck in a very different sort of underground. So, a short prayer at the shrine of claustrophobia, arms up and I am an eel wiggling over the slope, borrowed kneepads suddenly incredibly useful. The tunnel within a tunnel only continues for a few feet perhaps, but when I am halfway through and see Andy perched on the other side, the fact I am going for it fills me with loopy joy. I flop back into the water on the other side, laughing with indecorous dementedness. God, it feels good.

Again, the gang insist I swim first, capture all this river that is not river before it muddies, so that soon I am floating down what resembles two tunnels, one above and one below, so clear I could reach down through the water and touch it. I reach a wet crossroads, shafts to left, right and ahead. Here, the miners would have found a fault and chased it left and right in hope of finding a mineral vein. History says they failed. This was a non-mine, an expensive, hard-laboured birth that led to no profit. Except tonight, where we are the ones profiting. Ian unpacks his boxes, hands out flashguns like sweeties, reminding his helpmeets to keep the flashguns dry as they don't want to mess with 1500 volts. The other three wade off down side tunnels, to play the role of instant candles.

When I first met Andy and Ian on the open-mine tour mentioned earlier, we traipsed down a similar, though much drier, shaft deep into the heart of barytes-mining history. Once ensconced in the bowels, Andy lit a candle then asked us to turn off our headlamps. He explained that, in those times, tallow candles made from beef fat were expensive, so, on breaks, the candles were snuffed out and time passed in utter invisibility. Suddenly, we were reduced to a world of flicker, shadow and flare. A cliché to call it living history, but briefly, I had a sense of the ancestors breathing in a shaft nearby. Then he blew out the candle and the darkness of the world was with us and in us. It was an absolute black, the tint of a raven's wing without the telltale sheen. The moment was disturbed only by some annoying git fiddling with the screen on his phone. We have become addicted to the easy glare of electric, the comfort that light brings.

Here, as I half-wade, half-stroke the surface of this self-levelling pool, I am reminded how extraneous we are. More so, when I ask Ian about fish or bats and my words actually cause a flutter glimpsed in the corner of my eye, which resolves itself into flying annoyance as wings beat off down the right-hand tunnel, away from all that noise and chromatic confusion. I feel doubly blessed, swimming deep underground, and then finding that I am briefly sharing this space with a lesser horseshoe bat, for whom rock is a veritable soundboard and echo its A–Z.

The shot has been set. Mid-crossroads, I am on stage, water reflecting silver. I have to swim back and forth, my eyes blinking at the stark flash brightness, as Ian takes the picture over and over until, numbed by cold, my toes stop sending signals to my brain. Then we're done.

We wade a couple of hundred yards further in. Suddenly, our few feet of water become ten feet, a perfect infinity pool dropping away deep beneath our feet. It's like looking over a miniature abyss as, again, the water is so perfectly clear that we can see every tiny shard of stone picked out by our headlamps at the pool's bottom, all of it tinted blue. Here's the fact of deep water. As the light from our lamps, or if outside, the sun, hits the water, red and yellow light are absorbed in the upper layers, but blue is not. So, what we are seeing is not the pool in itself, but our electric interaction with it.

We talk about taking some more shots; I am keen to dive in but my body has begun its own small revolution. I am shaking all over and my teeth have started a peculiar clattering conversation that will not end well. I have swum in January waterfalls with no problems. However, that entry and exit is time-limited, the shock squeezed into an acceptable shortness. I've now been submerged for well over an hour in my summer wetsuit. All my fierce gladness is dripping away and the tunnel closes over my head, reminding me as I turn and stoop my aching way back that it's very unlikely there were ever any six-foot-eight miners.

It is extraordinary how moods can move in flux like water. The team tell me to lead the way and make my own pace. What was crystal round my waist is now slow-moving, hindering murk. Mineral-seamed ceilings press down too close for comfort. I can see how miners easily grew confused. Do I go left at this shaft, or right? Will that lead to a dead end? The roof fall I squeezed through so effortlessly on the way in now becomes an impassable mountain climb and the final, actual exit from the mine moves further away from me as I stumble in a panic towards it. I tell my body not to overreact. Who dies in South Shropshire? I live here, for God's sake. But that gap towards the up-top has never appeared so welcoming.

Ejected back out onto earth, I have survived. However, the evening is not over yet. We are twenty-five minutes' walk from the car and earlier Ian suggested I leave all my stuff there as the stroll would warm me up. I try to stop shaking all over and really don't feel good. The December night has never seemed less welcoming. At least there is no wind, but, flickering here and there through the trees, there is the orange glow of streetlamps and houses from the small town below. Do the residents know what we have done and where we have been as they sat tucked up in front of their fires and TVs? For once, I have stepped away from the vicarious viewing of a Michael Palin or David Attenborough programme and gone into a dark actuality. I did the thing I dreamed about.

The others are off to the pub and I really owe them a drink, but my body, at least now wrapped in warm dry clothes, is begging to sit in a hot car. My toes are still abroad and I'm not sure when or indeed if they will return. I give the gang, all members of the Shropshire Caving and Mining Club, my thanks and drive off. On the way home, on the last hill before I descend into our village, a hare appears on the high ridge road, sprinting straight towards me. Thankfully, she swerves from sight and I head for the warmth of hearth and family and the different, reassuring submersion of a hot bath.

Carding Mill Valley Reservoir, the Long Mynd

THIS MORNING BEGAN WELL, a trickle of light gently squeezing between banks of cloud; this flow of orange, this current of yellow, this tributary that begins the day high in the heavens then bursts over the sky, flooding the leaden dullness. The last few weeks have weighed down like the heavy mass of grey ore pickaxed from the down-deep shafts of South Shropshire. The urge to swim has gone from me, as if I'd never even known it, had disowned that sense of immersive possibility.

Up until breakfast, I had every desire to cancel the plan made with my friend and photographer Tom to risk the reservoir on the Long Mynd, whatever the weather was hammering home. Last night, I practised my whingeing as best I could, though Polly would have none of it, despite my warning her about my back, my poor circulation, the overall tiredness of December. To no avail. Thus Tom and I find ourselves driving through the great glacial

Carding Mill Valley Resevoir

mouth of Carding Mill Valley, this well-deserved bastion of the National Trust, beautiful Shropshire haven for ever rarer birds and hawks, flora and fauna. On this cold, bright, winter morning, the valley is also empty. We pass the café optimistically setting up for the day and cross the ford through the Ashbrook to head for the top car park, the palm of a gravelled hand centred on the great up-thrusting valleys of the Mynd. Steepness is all and we are just that bit too early as the sun gilds the uppermost reaches, but leaves these gouged valley bottoms still echoing with cold night and even chillier breezes funnelling through steep sides.

The path follows the brook and a series of small pools that formed the earlier reservoirs and drinking fountains of Church Stretton; until, at the head of the valley, an unnatural green slope rises precipitously, turfed-over architecture holding back and holding on to the rising spring water and falling rain to create one of the deepest artificial pools in Shropshire. At nine thirty in the morning, with the pool buried in shadow and a ground temperature under three degrees, we decide to wimp out for a while and chase the sun line.

Depositing rucksacks and wetsuits, we scramble up twisted sheep paths, trying to catch the day. Beside a wrinkled and contorted old hawthorn that has spread itself wide and low to survive the season's winds, we cross from the dark into brightness. Colour explodes. The dead bracken is no longer brown but fired with orange. A single wren bobs about on the stems of last summer's grass as we settle down to enjoy this brief interlude of geographical warmth. Hats, gloves, scarves are stowed as December is outgunned by the sun. The far hills of this undulating county are striated and stretched out in front of us. As the Long Mynd is so high up, there is the feeling of looking down on the landscape, of vantage points and the slight vertigo that massive vistas can produce.

However, we can't contemplate such views forever. We are here for a reason and it's time to get togged up. But the moment we clamber back down below the sun line, regret sets in. The temperature difference feels ridiculous, confirmed as we strip off and an arctic wind slaps my bare back. If Tom wasn't here, I would almost certainly have wimped out, but that choice is denied me. At least I have a slight delay as Tom decides to take some photos of me standing in the huge concrete outflow that is both ugly and stark, yet somehow honest in its function. The only access is round the edge of the lake, which means the two of us wading in up to our knees. The industrial result creates a lovely contrast, man and nature combined through the setting of concrete.

The old signs here used to proclaim all the terrible things that could happen if one went for a dip. However, all that has changed. I talked recently to Pete Carty, Countryside Manager for South Shropshire. The National Trust are very keen these days to get visitors out of doors and closer to nature. In consultation with their risk management team, hill-scrambling and tree-climbing are actively encouraged. Even better, the no-swim policy at this reservoir and some other sites has been reversed, with wild swimming supported so long as people are sensible, stay aware of the dangers and don't head out by themselves. The new signs are far more encouraging, setting out a proper welcome for all the reservoir has to offer. Excellent news!

Despite a good amount of neoprene between me and the reservoir, and despite thinking of myself as a hardened wild swimmer, the cold that courses down my toes and up my legs is to be respected. Tom has forgotten his wetsuit boots. He has no gloves and no hat. He is far more of a man than me. The time has come. Because we are blokes and there are two of us, it feels entirely appropriate to go a bit macho on our next steps and our commitment to the cause. We decide that the moment we are in up to our waists, and after a countdown of three, we have to dive in. Tom is up for it but I'm not so sure. As the slippery stone and concreted slope feels uncertain under my feet, and as the lake spreads before us, both uninviting and challenging, I begin the count.

We might be coddled and swaddled in rubber, but nothing can put to simile what the shock of diving into winter water is like. *Electric* would be a dull, sparkless description. Closer to capsizing off a boat in the North Sea, in a storm, in winter with little hope of shore or home or life again. Forgive the drama, but if there were any twittering birds in the bushes round the edge, they are now drowned out by our whimpers and screams. The second part of our macho mission is that we must swim out near the centre of the lake, where there is a huge, rusting iron column that formed part of the original waterworks. This is no dip, but a full-on, full-steam-ahead, open-throttle forging-out into the depths, followed by a scuttle back to shore. Toes have gone numb. The work of the wetsuit to warm the water between neoprene and skin is a scientific lie that does not work here. Tom has been swimming the front crawl, whereas I, as ever, rely on the tortoise-like breast stroke. So he wins by a few yards and I am still a little way out when I decide it should be shallow enough for me to stand. I forget the nature of this pool, where the banks naturally drop as steeply as the valley around, as that is what they were part of originally. I try to stand and nearly go under, out of my depth.

Of course there is panic, but the scramble to the shore is

complete. We are laughing and shivering, scrubbing frenziedly with towels as the sun is still miles away high up the valley walls and I am trying to disgorge myself from this stupidly sticky wetsuit and free my goose-pimpled, shaking body. All macho-ness is gone. We completed the challenge; the challenge is now to make blood flow in my feet again. Once changed, I jump up and down on the spot, run in circles, try anything to stop that itchy, painful sense of digit-loss. There is no feeling except ice, water, flow, the joy that in my actual madness I was far far from this place but oh how I have returned.

Before we head down the hill, I pause and turn back, can almost see myself sitting on the same bank one hot September lunchtime just over thirteen years ago when a phone call came. While I was out, the midwife had visited to bring us a home-birthing kit. It was close to the due date for the birth of our second child, but nothing had been expected to begin any time soon and Polly was happy for me to skive off for a swim so long as my mobile phone was switched on. Now apparently it was all action, but not labour. It had transpired that, over the course of a single week, Polly had been creating more and more amniotic fluid, far too much. In the midwife's words, as she vainly tried to search for head or bum, our baby was swimming around like a dolphin, one moment breech, the next transverse. Hospital was the only answer. So, I was summoned from that drowsy, après-bathe lolling to be all-round-useful chauffeur and useless husband as scans were done and checked. Yes, they showed that our soon-to-be-greeted son was not 'engaged' at all: his head should have been down, ready to dive into the new world. He shouldn't have been able to slip round with such ease. He was misbehaving, a mercurial Puck even before his first breath. When scanned, he was in feet-down breech position. Ten minutes later, an obstetrician with careful hands pronounced she was sure the baby had moved again, head down. If so, it was time to dam the escape routes while the going was good.

Intervention involved the use of a crochet hook implement to free the waters, drain the pool, force the trapped-cork sinking of a baby's head downwards. When that didn't work, drug inducements trickled in a slow current through Polly's arm until, six hours later, from all that water, from out of the same day I'd swum in the reservoir, life breathed into a boy with both cheek and charm. He was definitely a water boy.

Rhaeadr Mawddach, Wales

I HAVE AN INTIMATE RELATIONSHIP with the River Mawddach, which began on my and Polly's fifteenth wedding anniversary and the suggestion of a friend that we really should check out Barmouth sometime. We did, and thus began an affair that persists to this day, prompted by our first sight of the estuary as we turned off the Dolgellau road. That great wide expanse of water and sand, as if the mountains had been flattened by a steamroller, is rightly called a mouth, the lip of which contains the mostly wonderful and befitting grey stone Victorian architecture that makes up the town. As mentioned, our children have spent many holidays and wonderful weekends here. All of us have dipped in sea, estuary, tarn, lake and waterfall.

Many years ago, under the great railway bridge that connects south to north, my mate Gary and I rode his jet ski into the sunset, skimming the shallows in a petrol-fumed rush of speed as the day died into shadows and water became the launch pad for our flight. Gary was fearless and slightly mad as he swooped us like gulls into too tight corners and then beached us on a sandbank mid-river. I could not believe my luck, to be standing in the middle of the Afon Mawddach on a warm September evening, seeing the river from a new angle.

Today, another season, another year, and I am approaching the Mawddach from a very different viewpoint, higher on its journey, when it is still swaddled by great moss-clad forest. My daughter is home from her first term at university and on camera duty, as well as being up for a tramp through the trees. I made a decision when I rose this morning, at the beginning of a three-day write and swim trip: it was to say 'sod off' to seasonal affective disorder; to finally see through the advertising-more-than lie which insists happiness is only a plane-hop away and you too can be free of the grey jumblies. But today, with its rain both persistent and consistent and its cover of cloud complete, is just what the season ordered. Perhaps Buddhist acceptance is a truer path. Rather than wanting to turn from the weather, why not embrace it?

So here goes the optimistic traveller, thermos, sandwich and waterproof packed, out of Shropshire and into the high fastness of Wales, to the nature palace of Prince Cadwgan of Powys, who owned this land one thousand years ago. Think of the hawking, the deer, the wild boar and thrill of the green hunt! Now, we have moulded lumps of earth where mountain bikers become the modern stags leaping for the chase.

When we turn away from the town of Dolgellau and away from the sedate lower reaches of our river, the hills take over. In valleys, roads dominate, run straight as, well, as rivers. But higher up, they must kink and jink like hawks in their hunt for the source of the stream. The river is now channelled, and thus her energy

Rhaeadr Mawddach

is angry, all of the recent rainfall somersaulting over itself in a brown, peaty rush of gravity. We climb higher, happy to have the woods to ourselves, ready for the moment the road gives up the ghost, turns to track, then single footpath.

In the drizzle, the car is stowed, camera and swimwear packed, sandwiches gulped for energy as we head out and up, playing follow-my-leader with the river. How to find the waterfall? Sound and song will betray it.

This whole area was up until 1999 a working gold mine. I panned for gold in the heartlands of Alaska many years ago, my prize a bucket full of worthless grit. But this is already treasure for free. Sure, summer has its adherents, and I will admit beyond the bounds of these pages that, come the warm days, I try to submerge myself pretty much most afternoons that I can. However, this close to Christmas, each tree is covered in raindrop baubles, decked out in electric green moss. As for gifts, these await us round the corner.

I simply need to unwrap myself of clothes, don wet-boots and gloves, though the only wetsuit I have with me today is my skin as I get ready to sink into the moment. We have clambered through the heart of the old industrial workings. Big, rusting metal pipes everywhere, and buildings that have carelessly lost roof, windows and purpose. All is lichen, crumble and slowly subsuming back into nature. Here, two rivers meet and there is a rare treat for wild swimmers – two waterfalls for the price of one. However, Pistyll y Cain is not for me today. The force of the fall sends spray a good fifty metres and the current that churns round the receiving whirlpool looks not just dangerous, but potentially fatal. I know my limits.

Rhaeadr Mawddach it is then. Roz balances on the lower

rocks, working out the correct camera settings to seek me out in the middle of all that white spume. I am further up, determined to jump in and swim round the edge of this giant pool, which must be at least forty yards across. Under the falls themselves, the current appears to be spinning and at the far edge, where the waters spill downhill, the acceleration is a power rush, river in a hurry to the sea. I have no desire to encounter either, and must find the quieter spots where wildness is slow enough not to tighten its grip and tumble me out of control.

At least the clouds have done us a favour, acting as insulation, making the late December afternoon almost warm. I slip my way over the edge, my feet trying to find footholds, work out where shore ends and depth begins. Until suddenly I am swimming, or rather I'm not, as I edge round the pool, the current so strong I hardly move, flailing like a butterfly on a pin. Not only this, but some deep instinct prevented me from diving in and for that I am grateful. There were the remains of a metal rail near the edge of the water and I have just found out that the said metal has a nasty relative hidden underwater which I have to drag myself round. This is not breast stroke as we know it; more of an eel-like desperate slither, bumping into hidden rocks, trying not to grimace, and hoping hard that I'll make it back to shore.

Of course I do, and stand up feeling fierce and bonkers-brave, saluting the waterfall and giving thanks to the gods of rain and spring-burst. I get out, dry off, but the urge is still in me. I ask Roz if I should just be happy and stop now. She says yes, stop, concerned about currents. Do not try this at home. And yet it is not enough. Not quite. So I clamber back in, bend my knees and gain myself a proper dunking, let Mawddach, the rocks, the mountains, the rain, the clouds, the estuary, the drinking mouth, all of it wash over me on the day I decided to stop fighting winter.

The poet Gerard Manley Hopkins, whose lilt and language were filled with sprung rhythm and the bounce of nature, knew this river well:

> The Mawddach, how she trips! though throttled
>
> If floodtide teeming thrills her full...

This moment is precious. My lovely Rosalind, with whom I have shared so many adventures, is now tumbling down her own fall into new life. She has returned from her first term somehow different. Vulnerable, confident, changed. All the mercurial aspects of water, of her spirit, and of our family are contained here and now, to make this not just a day for wild swimming, but chat and laughter and heart-to-heart. Bright blessing to our grey days, the girl who surfed the surge of different waters eighteen years ago.

I too have changed this year. M, the counsellor provided by the NHS when I was at greatest need, has said that I am better, that I don't need her listening ear any more. There, in that series of safe sessions, I risked unclear waters, mapped out the currents of my broken history and somehow, finally, found a way to stay afloat despite the whirlpool's lure. To say I am grateful for the harbour would be understatement, for here I have wept my own waterfall and never been judged. She tells me that the service is under threat and I worry that when another troubled soul comes for help some day soon, he or she will not find such succour, that government cuts will do exactly that – cut to the quick. With imminent job losses, who will be there to counsel future sufferers? While there is no shame in such illness, shame on the politicians for their arrogant lack of concern. At least in some small way, through what I write and speak, I might reach out and tell them, those lost ones in the future, that they are not alone.

The man who shivered in the shower, and found a humid swimming pool a threat, has regained the leaping urge. Accompanied by the sound of tumble and roar, I walk away from the waterfall, having learned the friendship of all seasons. Cold is not a battle, but the fiercest joy; water not the drowning enemy, but the friend I lost once and found again.

Taking a dip at Nantcol

DAD WENT SWIMMING RECENTLY – a brief, mad dash in and out of the freezing hillside pool. I crouched on the rocks above with my camera in hand, trying to frame the moment, to capture him in the green cocoon of running water. I squinted through the eyepiece as he squealed. The winter stream was bitterly chilly, but I forced him to stay until I could focus and click. As he jumped out and reached for the towel I had a brief snatch of elation, of realising quite how special these small moments still are.

A year ago my dad wasn't dipping so much as a toe into cold water. This was unusual for a man who celebrated the delights of mountain streams and plunge pools regardless of season or temperature. The other three of us often watched as he slid in and out of lakes or rivers, his long legs kicking up as he laughed with the adrenaline rush. Roger Deakin's *Waterlog* was his guiding text, the outdoors his cathedral. Then the swimming stopped. Long walks, days out and that fascination with the beating heart of forests and hills gradually disappeared too.

Depression was the diagnosis – the word he was given to explain why he could no longer function; the word that was offered to my brother and me to justify why our dad would be moving temporarily out of our home and into hospital; the word handed to my mum to help her understand why her husband's eyes were empty. That word has become misappropriated and misunderstood. It is a clinical term, describing an illness that debilitates both mind and body. It is not interchangeable with sadness, despondency or any of the other more easily defined emotions. 'Sadness' doesn't hang like fog in the living room for six months. It doesn't do justice to the man whose head was full of terror, hands trembling as he ate, speech devoted only to paranoia and apologies. 'Sadness' wasn't what created an impassable void between our father and the figure that sat on the sofa all day. This shape looked like dad, but had none of his curiosity or humour. It huddled reading trashy books and filling out sudokus day after day as we tried to coax *him* out. I imagined the real man outside somewhere, sculling up and down a river or strolling through a field at twilight, as he used to do. The outdoors scared this replacement. When we went away to visit friends he pleaded with us to let him out of the car, to leave him behind, to let him walk back home. Our house was a cave, with everything beyond the walls and windows threatening.

Severe depression took all that my dad loved and lived for, and warped it. The chemical imbalance in his brain made literature unreadable and the landscape unreachable and terrifying. For him, each stretch of water was no longer an embrace, but a place filled with possible dangers: broken glass and barbed wire waiting at the bottom or hidden currents that might pull us all under. He didn't need the adrenaline from jumping in the sea, his system already full of it from the constant horror and panic of 'fight or flight' as he sat on the sofa. He tried to fold himself away there, but couldn't curl small enough to pass unseen. We saw, and it hurt.

Depression is a wound of sorts. The hope is that it can eventually heal – although the process of recovery may be one of complications and setbacks. Getting better is also a different process for everyone. The possibility of my dad's return became clear on the afternoon he agreed to join me for a walk. Our conversation was stilted, but the steps were progress. Like a tide, the extent of the following revival varied from day to day. He moved from activity to monosyllables as moods shifted. But if the stroll was a first sign, then the revisiting of a favourite river was a decisive signal. It's not melodramatic to say that when he was so ill, neither my mum nor I could imagine him ever swimming again. The idea was incompatible with the reality we had watched for months. Nonetheless, there he was – hollering with as much energy as remembered, lips grinning beneath a striped beanie hat.

It now strikes me that his illness left him stuck at the bottom of a silted lake. We wanted, desperately, to catch him with hooks, suddenly yank him from the depths – dredge him up in an instant. Instead it was an agonising process of waiting for the dark liquid to drain away, drop by drop.

That liquid is now not dark, but clear. The riverbed is sandy and covered in stones. Dad made up for lost time through cycling, writing and taking me on six-mile walks. Although it is now cold, he still retains this spark – a desire to fill himself up with life and the joy of being here. Whenever he now steps into a mountain plunge pool, with breeze ruffling leaves, it is an act of celebration. A celebration of swimming; of the human ability to suffer and recover; of the wonder to be found in days out and other activities; of the bonds between family; and of the relationship with the outdoors.

We all push forward, taking it one stroke at a time.

> What would the world be, once bereft
>
> Of wet and of wildness? Let them be left,
>
> O let them be left, wildness and wet;
>
> Long live the weeds and the wilderness yet.

GERARD MANLEY HOPKINS, 'Inversnaid'

At the Rhaeadr Du waterfall

Acknowledgements

I would like to thank Pete Carty of the National Trust for all his advice and suggestions; Tom Middleton for his support for all things *Dip*-related and swim fun; and Ian Cooper with the Shropshire Mining and Caving group for taking me deep down underneath Shropshire. There are many other acquaintances, friends and colleagues along the way who have been more than happy to share their water and wildlife knowledge, and I hope I have named them properly within the text – thank you! Much gratitude to Uli and Eugene as ever; to all the team at Rider for seeing *Dip*'s potential; and to Sue for her thoughtful editing. Above all, I want to thank my daughter, Roz, for her superb photography and sharing many of our trips out, and my wife, Polly, for her editorial and re-writing skills and her unwavering support, which made *Dip* possible.

The Afterword 'Wild Swimming' by Rosalind Jana first appeared as a guest blog on *Young Minds* in December 2012 (www.youngminds.org.uk).

All photos © Rosalind Jana and Andrew Fusek Peters, except 'Carding Mill Valley Reservoir, The Long Mynd' © Tom Middleton, page 225, and 'Semi-Submerged Mine Shaft, South Shropshire' © Ian Cooper, page 217